AMERICAN SLAVE STORIES

True Stories of Slavery in the American South

From

Slave Narratives: A Folk History of Slavery in the United States From
Interviews with Former Slaves

Work Projects Administration

ISBN-13:
978-1976465130

ISBN-10:
1976465133

Charlie Aarons

Personal contact with Uncle Charlie Aarons
Oak Grove, Alabama
—Written by Mary A. Poole

HE LOVED YOUNG MARSTER JOHN

Some friends driving to Oak Grove, Ala., gave the writer the opportunity on August 4th to interview an old ex-slave, Charlie Aarons, who is quite venerable in appearance, and who, when asked his age, replied:

"Madam I don't know but I sure been 'round here long time", and when asked how old he was at the time of the Surrender he answered:

"I was a man able to do a man's work so I 'spects I was eighteen or twenty years old."

Uncle Charlie, as he is known among his own color and the white people who know him, told the writer he was born at Petersburg Va., and his parents, Aaron and Louisa, were owned by a Mr. J.H. White, who had a store in the city, but no plantation. His parents had three children, two boys and one girl, and when Uncle Charlie was about ten years of age, he was sold by Mr. White to a speculator named Jones who brought him to Mobile. He recalled being placed on the block, at the slave mart on Royal and State streets, and the anxiety of hearing the different people bidding for him, and being finally sold to a Mr. Jason Harris, who lived near Newton Station in Jasper County, Miss.

Uncle Charlie never saw or heard of his parents or brother and sister again and never knew what became of them.

Uncle Charlie said Mr. Harris was a pretty rough master, and somewhat close. All rations were weighed out and limited. He had a white overseer and a negro driver, who was the meanest of all.

Mr. Jason Harris had about sixty slaves, and a large plantation of a hundred acres, the men and women worked in the fields from six to six, except on Saturday, when they had half day holiday to clean up generally.

The home of the Harris family was a large two story house and the quarters were the regular log cabins with clay chimneys. They cooked in their cabins, but during the busy season in the fields their dinners were sent out to them each slave having his own tin pail marked with his name. Water would be sent out in a barrel mounted on an ox cart.

The old men and women looked after the children of the slaves while their parents worked in the fields.

When the writer asked Uncle Charlie, if his master or mistress ever taught him to read or write, he smiled and said:

"No, Madam, only to work".

When asked if they had any special festivities at Christmas or any other holiday, he replied:

"No, we had no special jolifications".

Saturday nights they would sing and dance in the quarters and have prayer meetings, then on some Sundays, they would hitch up the mules to a big wagon and all go to the white folks church: and again there would be camp meetings held and the slaves from all the surrounding plantations would attend, going to same in these large wagons, sometimes having four mules to a wagon. They then would have a jolly time along the way, singing and calling to one another, and making friends.

Uncle Charlie, said, he drove many a load of cotton in the large mule wagons from Newton Station to Enterprise, Mississippi.

When asked if that wasn't a chance to run away, he replied:

"Git away, why Madam, those nigger dogs would track you and all you got was a beating."

Uncle Charlie seemed to look off in the distance and said: "You know, Madam, I never saw a slave rebuked until I came to Mississippi," and I just couldn't understand at first, but he grinned and said: "Lordy, Madam, some of those niggers were onery, too, and a nigger driver was a driver sure enough."

When the Master's son John Harris went to war, Charlie went with him as his body guard, and when asked what his duties were, he replied:

"I looked after Marster John, tended the horses and the tents. I recalls well, Madam, the siege of Vicksburg."

The writer then asked him if he wasn't afraid of the shot and shell all around him.

"No, Madam," he replied, "I kept way in the back where the camp was, for I didn't like to feel the earth trembling 'neath my feet, but you see, Madam, I loved young Marster John, and he loved me, and I just had to watch over that boy, and he came through all right."

Uncle Charlie said when they were told the Yankees were coming through from their headquarters in Meridian, Mississippi, and warned of their raids, they all made to the swamps and staid until they had passed on, but that the Yankees did not disturb the Jason Harris plantation.

After the Surrender Charlie came to Mobile and worked at the Yankee Camp, living in the quarters located in Holly's Garden. He drove their wagons and was paid $14.00 a month and his keep. After his discharge he worked on steamboats and followed different lines of work, being employed for several years at Mr. M.L. Davis' saw mill, and is at present living on the Davis place at Oak Grove, Ala., an old Southern home, with quarters originally built for the employees of the mill and still known as the "quarters", and like other ante-bellum homes they have their private burying ground on the place.

Uncle Charlie was married four times, but now a widower. He had four children, two boys who are dead, and two girls, one Carrie Johnson, a widow, living in Kushla, Ala., and the other, Ella Aarons, a grass widow, living in Mobile, Ala.

Uncle Charlie says he saw Jeff. Davis as an old man, after the war at Mississippi City, Miss., and then his face lit up, and he said; "Wait a minute, Madam, I saw another president, let me think,—Yes, Madam I saw President Grant. He came through Mobile from New Orleans, and my! there was a big parade that day."

When asked about Abraham Lincoln, Uncle Charlie thought awhile, and answered:

"According to what was issued out in the Bible, there was a time for slavery, people had to be punished for their sin, and then there was a time for it not to be, and the Lord had opened a good view to Mr. Lincoln, and he promoted a good idea."

When he was asked about Booker T. Washington he replied:

"It was traversed out to him until the white folks took part with him and helped him carry on."

Uncle Charlie thinks the present day folks are bad and wicked, and dont realize anything like the old folks.

Charlie is a Baptist, became one when he sought the Lord and thinks all people should be religious.

Anthony Abercrombie

Interview with Anthony Abercrombie
—Susie R. O'Brien, Uniontown, Alabama

OLD JOE CAN KEEP HIS TWO BITS

Uncle Ant'ny sat dozing in the early morning sunshine on his rickety front porch. He is a thin little old man with patches of white wool here and there on his bald head, and an expression of kindness and gentleness on his wrinkled old face.

As I went cautiously up the steps, which appeared none too safe, his cane which had been leaning against his chair, fell to the floor with a clatter. He awoke with a start and began fumbling around for it with his trembling and bony hands.

"Uncle Ant'ny, you don't see so well, do you?" I asked as I recovered the stick for him. "No ma'am, I sho' don't," he replied. "I ain't seed none outen one of my eyes in near 'bout sixty years, and de doctor say I got a catalac on de yuther one; but I knows you is white folks. I always is been puny, but I reckon I does purty well considerin' I is a hundred years old."

"How do you know you are that old?" I inquired of him. Without hesitation he answered, "I knows I's dat old 'cause my mistis put it down in de Bible. I was born on de fourth day and I was a full growed man when de war come on in '61.

"Yassum, my mind kinder comes and goes, but I can always 'member 'bout slave'y time. Hits de things what happen in dese days dat's so easy for me to disremember. I b'longed to Marster Jim Abercrombie. His plantation was 'bout sixteen miles north of Marion in Bibb county. When his son, young Jim, ma'ied, old Marse Jim give me to him and he fetched me to Perry county.

"No'm, old marster didn't go to war 'ca'se he was corrupted; he was deaf in bofe ears and couldn't see good nuther. But he didn't care much 'bout me 'caze I was puny like and warn't much 'count in de field.

"My mistis, Miss Lou, was raisin' me up to be a carriage driver, an' she was jes' as good to me as she could be. She useta dose me up wid castor oil, jimson root, and dogwood tea when I'd be feelin' po'ly, and she'd always take up for me when Marse Jim get in behind me 'bout somep'n. I reckon though I was a purty worrisome nigger in dem days; always gettin' in some kind of mischief.

"O yassum, I useta go to meetin'. Us niggers didn't have no meetin' house on de plantation, but Marse Jim 'lowed us to build a brush arbor. Den two years atter de surrender I took consideration and j'ined up wid de Lawd. Dat's how come I live so long. De Lawd done told me, 'Antn'y, you got a hundred and twenty miles to trabel. Dat mean you gwine to live a hundred and twenty years, if you stay on de straight an' narrow road. But if you don't, you gotter go jes' de same as all de yuthers.'"

"Tell me something about your master's slaves and his overseers," I asked of him.

"Well," he said, "Marse Jim had 'bout three hundred slaves, and he hed one mighty bad overseer. But he got killed down on de bank of de creek one night. Dey never did find out who killed him, but Marse Jim always b'lieved de field han's done it. 'Fore dat us niggers useta go down to de creek to wash ourselves, but atter de overseer got killed down dar, us jes' leave off dat washin', 'cause some of 'em seed de overseer's ha'nt down dar floatin' over de creek.

"Dar was another ha'nt on de plantation, too. Marse Jim had some trouble wid a big double-j'inted nigger named Joe. One day he turn on Marse Jim wid a fence rail, and Marse Jim had to pull his gun an' kill him. Well, dat happen in a skirt of woods what I get my lightwood what I use to start a fire. One day I went to dem same woods to get some 'simmons. Another nigger went wid me, and he clumb de tree to shake de 'simmons down whilst I be pickin' 'em up. 'Fore long I heared another tree shakin' every time us shake our tree, dat other tree shake too, and down came de 'simmons from it. I say to myself, 'Dat's Joe, 'cause he likes 'simmons too.' Den I grab up my basket and holler to de boy in de tree, 'nigger turn loose and drap down from dar, and ketch up wid me if you can. I's leavin' here right now, 'cause Old Joe is over dar gettin' 'simmons too.'

"Den another time I was in de woods choppin' lightwood. It was 'bout sundown, and every time my ax go 'whack' on de lightwood knot, I hear another whack 'sides mine. I stops and lis'ens and don't hear nothin'. Den I starts choppin' ag'in I hears de yuther whacks. By dat time my houn' dog was crouchin' at my feets, wid de hair standin' up on his back and I couldn't make him git up nor budge.

"Dis time I didn' stop for nothin'. I jes' drap my ax right dar, an' me and dat houn' dog tore out for home lickety split. When us got dar Marse Jim was settin' on de porch, an' he say: 'Nigger, you been up to somep'n you got no business. You is all outen breath. Who you runnin' from?' Den I say: 'Marse Jim, somebody 'sides me is choppin' in yo' woods, an' I can't see him. And Marse Jim, he say: 'Ah, dat ain't nobody but Ole Joe. Did he owe you anythin'?' An' I say: 'Yassah, he owe me two-bits for helpin' him shuck corn.' 'Well,' Marse Jim say, 'don't pay him no mind: it jes' Old Joe come back to pay you.'

"Anyhow, I didn' go back to dem woods no mo'. Old Joe can jes' have de two-bits what he owe me, 'cause I don't want him follerin' 'roun' atter me. When he do I can't keep my mind on my business."

Nannie Bradfield

Interview with Nannie Bradfield
—Susie R. O'Brien, Uniontown, Alabama

WHAT I KEER ABOUT BEIN' FREE?

Nannie Bradfield is a fat little old woman almost as broad as she is long, with a pleasant face and a broad smile which displays white teeth still good at the age of eighty-five. She lives alone in a dilapidated cabin which rests in a clump of trees by the side of the railroad. The sagging roof is patched with pieces of rusty tin of many shapes and sizes.

"Nannie," I said, "aren't you afraid to live here alone?"

"How come I be skeered? Ain't nobody gwine bother me lessen it be a spirit, and dey don't come 'roun' 'cep'n on rainy nights, den all you got to do is say 'Lawd have mercy! What you want here,' and dey go 'way and leave you 'lone.

"Any how I's gittin' pretty old and I won't be here so ve'y much longer so I jes' as well start gittin' 'quainted wid de spirits."

"Tell me something about yourself and your family, Nannie," I said. "Dere ain't nothin' much to tell 'cep I was born in slav'y times and I was 'bout twelve year old in May when 'mancipation come. My Pa and Ma b'longed to Mars James and Miss Rebecca Chambers. Dey plantation was jes' on de aidge of town and dat's what I was born. Mars James' son William was in de war and old Miss would send me to town whar all de sojers tents was, to tote sompen good to eat to dem. I don't 'member much 'bout de war 'cep de tents and de bum shells shootin'. I was little and couldn't do much but I waited on Miss Liz'beth, my young Miss, and waited on table, toted battie cakes and sich like. No ma'am I don't know nothin' 'tall 'bout de patterollers or de Klu Kluxers but I know all 'bout de conjer doctors. Dey sho' kin fix you. Dey kin take yo' garter or yo stockin' top an drap it in runnin' water and make you run de res' of yo' life, you'll be in a hurry all de time, and if dey gits holt of a piece of de seat of yo' draw's dey sprinkles a little conjer powder on it and burns it den you can't never set down in no peace. You jes' like you settin' on a coal of fiah 'till you git somebody to take de spell offen you."

"Nannie, were you glad when the war was over and you were free?"

"What I keer 'bout bein' free? Didn't old Marster give us plenty good
sompin to eat and clo's to wear? I stayed on de plantation 'til I mah'ied. My
old Miss give me a brown dress and hat. Well dat dress put me in de
country, if you mah'ie in brown you'll live in de country."

"'Marry in brown you'll live out of town?'" I quoted. "Dat's it—my
remembrance ain't so good and I fergits.

"No ma'am, I ain't got no chillun, but Bradfield had plenty un um, I was
his fouf wife. He died 'bout three years ago and he done well to live dat
long wid all dem wimmens to nag him. De Bible say it's better to climb on
top of the house and set, den to live inside wid a naggin' 'oman."

Emma Chapman

Interview with Emma Chapman
—Mary A. Poole

Living in a small room in the rear of a house at 361 Augusta Street, Mobile, Alabama, the writer located an interesting ex-slave, Emma Chapman, who when first approached was somewhat reticent. I soon learned I had arrived just as she was ready to have her breakfast, which consisted of bread and coffee, and insisted she eat first and talk afterwards, as she had made just about enough fire in the open fireplace to boil the coffee.

While she followed my suggestion I glanced about the room and found it very neat and tidy and an unusually comfortable looking double bed, a mirrored door chifferobe and two trunks, one rocking chair and a couple of straight chairs, a table containing all cooking utensils and food containers. The walls were covered with sheets of manilla wrapping paper, tacked on, and part of the ceiling patched with odds and ends of corrugated paper. Emma is small in stature, of light complexion with greying hair arranged in neat braids around her head, very clean in appearance.

Emma said she was about 13 years of age at the time of the surrender, and that she was born on the plantation of Rev. Mr. Montgomery Curry of Charleston, S.C. When she was about 3 years of age Mr. Curry moved to Pickens County, Alabama, about 5 miles from Carrollton and 8 miles from Pickenville. When I asked why they moved to Alabama, Emma laughed, and said they expected to find money growing on trees in Alabama, and that she as a child came near being "snake bit" many a time, digging around the roots of old trees, trying to find money.

Rev. Montgomery Curry, said Emma, was married to Ann Haynie, whose parents were Aaron and Francis Hudson Haynie, and Emma's grandmother was Lucy Linier, who was born in Virginia and was sold to Mr. Haynie to pay a debt. Lucy Linier was nurse for his daughter Ann and when she married Mr. Curry, she brought Lucy with her to her new home. The Currys had three children, a boy and two girls, and it was Lucy Linier's daughter, Patsy, who acted as their nurse.

The home of Rev. and Mrs. Montgomery Curry was a two-story log house with wide open hall running the entire length of the house and with rooms opening off either side. The kitchen was out a short distance from the main house, with the dairy between the two, under a large hickory tree.

The slave quarters were also built of logs, with space between for a shed room and small garden plot and a few chickens. The slave women did not go to the fields on Saturday as that was their day to clean up around their homes. They usually washed their clothes at night and hung them on the bushes where they were left to dry in the sunshine, maybe a couple of days, as no one could or would disturb them.

Rev. Montgomery Curry was a Baptist preacher and had no overseer, except Lucy Linier and her husband, Emma's grandparents, who kept a supervision over the slaves about 40 in number. There was no whipping allowed on the Curry plantation, and after the death of Reverend Curry, Mrs. Ann Curry (his widow) ran the plantation under the same system. The patrollers had no jurisdiction over the Curry slaves, they were given permits by the Currys to go and come, and Emma said if one of those patrollers whipped one of "ole Miss's slaves, she would have sure sued them.

Emma laughingly said the slaves on other plantations always said the Curry slaves were "free niggers," as they could always get permits, and had plenty to eat and milk to drink. The slaves cooked their breakfasts in their own cabins, but dinner and supper was cooked in the kitchen and each came with their pan to be filled and had their own gourds which were grown on the place to drink their milk and of which they could have full and plenty.

During the war they cooked for the Confederate soldiers encamped nearby and great quantities were prepared. Emma was one of those delegated to carry the food to the camp. All she ever saw of the Yankees were two who stopped at the house and asked for something to eat. Mrs. Montgomery invited them in and served the best she had. One of the men wanted to take the last mule she had and the other said "No, Mrs. Montgomery is a widow and from the appearance of her slaves she has treated them well."

Mrs. Montgomery told them that someone had stolen her saddle horse and the soldier who had remonstrated with the other replied: "Madam, your saddle horse will be returned in three weeks," and sure enoug, one night about midnight they heard a horse whinny and Emma's grandfather said "there is old Spunk," and there was old Spunk waiting outside.

Emma said the first whipping she ever had, was after the Surrender, given her by her own father when they left Alabama and went to live near Columbus, Miss.

She had always lived in the house with the "old Miss" and her young Miss, and when she had to leave them, she cried and so did they.

Her grandmother Lucy Linier nursed "Miss Ann"; Lucy's daughter Patsy nursed "Miss Ann's" children, and was the special property of Fannie Montgomery Curry, who married a Mr. Sidney Lipscomb and whose children Emma helped to look after, so the three generations were interwoven.

Emma only wishes she could go back to plantation days. All her trials and suffering came after she left "Ole Miss," and went to live with her father and mother, George and Patsy Curry, who had fourteen children and of which Emma was the eldest. Her father who was a quadroon in cast was cruel to his family, and especially so to her. He made her work like a man, cutting timber, splitting rails, digging, planting and all work of the farm.

Now, Emma is the only member of her family left. She married three times, having only two children, a girl and a boy, these by her last husband, Frank Chapman, now dead, and Emma has no knowledge of her children's whereabouts. She gave them an education so they could write to her if they wanted to. The girl married and left Mobile, the boy went to Chicago, was chauffeur for some rich folks. His last letter several years ago, in which he enclosed $25.00, stated he was going on a trip to Jerusalem with one of the young men of the family.

Hattie Clayton

Interview with Hattie Clayton
—Preston Klein

DE YANKS DRAPPED OUTEN DE SKY

'Aunt' Hattie Clayton said, "I'se gittin' erroun' de ninety notch, honey, an' I reckon de Kingdom ain't fur away."

She lives in a tiny cabin not far from Opelika. Her shoulders are bent; her hair gray, but she still does a large amount of housework. She likes to sit on the tumbledown front porch on summer afternoons, plying her knitting needles and stretching her aged legs in the warm sunlight.

"'Twas a long time ago, honey," she observed when talk of slavery days was brought up, "but I 'members as ef 'twas yestidy. My ol' mistus was de Widder Day. She owned a plantation clos't to Lafayette an' she was mighty good to us niggers.

"Ol' Mistus boughten me when I was jus' a little tyke, so I don't 'member 'bout my pappy an' mammy.

"Honey, I 'members dat us little chilluns didn't go to de fiel's twel us was big 'nuff to keep up a row. De oberseer, Marse Joe Harris, made us work, but he was good to us. Ol' Mistus, she wouldn't let us wuk whin it was rainin' an' cold."

Asked about pleasures of the old plantation life, she chuckled and recalled:

"I kin heah de banjers yit. Law me, us had a good time in dem days. Us danced most eb'ry Sattidy night an' us made de rafters shake wid us foots. Lots o' times Ole Missus would come to de dances an' look on. An' whin er brash nigger boy cut a cute bunch uv steps, de menfolks would give 'im a dime or so.

"Honey, us went t' de church on a Sundays. I allus did lak singin' and I loved de ol' songs lak, 'Ol' Ship of Zion,' an' 'Happy Land.' Ol' Mistus useter take all de little scamps dat was too little for church an' read de Book to dem under de big oak tree in de front yahd."

"Aunt Hattie," she was asked, "do you remember anything about the War between the States?"

"You mean de Yankees, honey?"

"Yes, the Yankees."

Her coal black face clouded.

"Dey skeered us nearly to death," she began. "Dey drap right outen de sky. Ol' Mistus keep hearin' dey was comin', but dey didn't nebber show up. Den, all ter once, dey was swarmin' all ober de place wid deir blue coats a-shinin' an' deir horses a'rarin'.

"Us chilluns run en hid in de fence corners en' behin' quilts dat was hangin' on de line. An' honey, dem Yankees rid deir horses rat onto Ol' Mistus flower beds. Dey hunted de silver, too, but us done hid dat.

"I 'members dey was mad. Dey sot de house a-fire an' tuk all de vittals dey could fin'. I run away an' got los', an' whin I come back all de folks was gone."

'Aunt' Hattie said she "wint down de big road an' come to a lady's house where she remained until she married.

"Us moved to Lafayette an' den to Opelika," she concluded, "an' I bin' here eber since."

She lives with one of her numerous granddaughters now. She finds her great happiness in "de promise" and the moments when she can sit in the shade and dip her mind back into memory.

Tildy Collins

Interview with Tildy Collins
—Susie R. O'Brien, Uniontown, Alabama

In the Negro section of Uniontown, locally known as "Rabbit Yard"
(named by the Negroes themselves), lives "Aunt Tildy" Collins, a typical
"black mammy" of orthodox type. She is a talkative old soul, running over
with slavery tales and greatly beloved by a wide range of acquaintances
among both races. Although eighty-four summers have passed over her
snow-white head, Aunt Tildy's spirit is unconquered by time and her
physical activity is truly remarkable for her age. She does her own
housework and cares for her home without assistance. In front of her one-
room cabin is a neat garden of vegetables and flowers combined, with
morning glories trained carefully over the fence nearly all the way around.
There is a saying in the South, that cotton will grow better for a Negro
than for any other race, and this might well be extended to include
morning glories in Aunt Tildy's case; since none in Uniontown are quite
so fine in growth or brilliance of coloring.

Like nearly all old Negroes, Aunt Tildy goes to sleep very readily. She
was dozing in a rocker on her small porch, while the scent of wood smoke
and the odor of boiling vegetables issued from the cabin. An iron pot,
hanging from a crane in the fireplace, sending forth clouds of steam and an
appetizing aroma. She clings to old fashioned equipment and disdains a
stove for cooking. Her "biled" vegetables or meats in the hanging pot, with
baked potatoes and "pone" bread from the oven make up a meal that
leaves little to be desired, as many visitors who have shared her repasts
well know.

As the gate squeaked, Aunt Tildy awoke with a start and a smile.

"Come in, white folks, I was jes' a-settin' here waitin' for my greens to
bile, an' I musta drapped off to sleep. Set down in dat cheer right dar, an'
tek off your hat; you sho' is lookin' well, an' I'se proud to see you.

"Yas, ma'am, I sho' was borned in slavery times, an' I wish to Gawd I
could git now what I useter hab den, 'caze dem was good times for de
black folks. Dese free niggers don't know what 'tis to be tuk good keer of.

"Co'se I means dat! I was borned on a big plantation near 'bout to Linden, an' my Ole Marster was name Harris, yassum, Dick Harris, an' my Ole Mistis was Miss Mandy. Bofe dey boys fit in de wah, an' I 'members when dey went off wid de sojers, ole Mistis she cry an' hug dem boys an' kiss 'em goodbye, an' dey was gone a long time. I was a leetle gal whenst dey went to de wah, an' I was mos' a grown 'oman when dey come home, an' dey bofe had whiskers. Young Massa Richard he limpin' an' look mighty pale, an' dey say he been wounded an' stay in prison on Mister Johnson's island, summuz up de ribber; but Marse Willis, he look all right, 'cep'in' whiskers. Ole Marster had a big house, an' dat same house standin' dar right now. Us had plenty to eat an' plenty to wear, an' dat's mo'n what some folks got now.

"Ole Marster was good to all he niggers, an' my pappy and mammy bofe belonged to him. Dey was a slave-yard in Uniontown, an' ev'y time a spec'later cum wid a lot of new niggers, Ole Marster he buy four or five niggers, an' dat's how he come to buy my pappy, atter de spec'later brung him an' a whole passel of niggers from North C'lina. My mammy here already 'long to Ole Marster. Her was borned his'n.

"Sometime a no 'count nigger tek an' runned erway; but de oberseer, he put de houn's on he track, an' dey run him up a tree, an' de oberseer fetch him back nex' mawnin', all tuckerd out, an' he' glad to stay home for a spell an' 'have hese'f. Ole Marster had a good oberseer, too. 'Cose he wan't no quality, lak Ole Marster an' Ole Mistis, but he was a good, kin' man an' he didn't hab no trouble on de whole plantation.

"Us alluz had a Chris'mus tree in de quarter, jes' lak de white folks an' dey was presents for ev'ybody—nobody wan't lef' out, big or little. Dere was a meetin' house on de plantation an' Ole Marster had a rule dat all de chilluns had to go to Sunday school soon as dey was big 'nuff, an' dey had to go in clean white clo'se, too. Us chilluns hate to see Sunday come, 'caze Mammy an' Granmammy dey wash us an' near 'bout rub de skin off gittin' us clean for Sunday school, an' dey comb our heads wid a jimcrow. You ain't neber seed a jimcrow? Hit mos' lak a card what you card wool wid. What a card look lak? Humph! Missy, whar you been raise—ain't neber seed a card? Dat jimcrow sho' did hurt, but us hadder stan' hit, an' sometimes atter all dat, Mammy she wrap our kinky hair wid t'read an' twis' so tight us's eyes couldn't hardly shet.

"My Granmammy, her de head cook 'oman at de big house, an' us had to mine her lak us did Mammy. I ho'p Granmammy in de kitchen, atter I got big 'nuff an' she sho' did keep me humpin'. Chilluns had to mine dey olders in dem days. Dey wan't lak dey is now, don't mine nobody, not eben dey Pa.

"When de surrender come, Ole Marster he tole all de niggers dey was free now, an' some was glad an' some was sorry an' welst dey might be sorry, iffen dey knowed what a hard time dey goner had knockin' 'roun' de worl' by deyself; no Ole Marster an' no Ole Mistis ter look atter 'em an' feed 'em when dey sick an' when dey well. Look lak ter me, when de surrender parted de white folks an' de black folks, it hurt 'em bofe. Dey oughter be tergedder, jes' lak de Good Lord 'tended dey be."

Aunt Tildy sighed deeply and, gazing afar off, said: "Iffen Ole Marster was livin' now, I'd be all right an' not hafter worry 'bout nuffin."

In spite of her eighty-four years, Aunt Tildy makes her living as a mid-wife and serves as a "doctor man" in cases of minor ailments; but her practice is so closely interwoven with "conju'in'" that it is difficult to say which is the more important to her. For example: she prescribes wearing matches in the hair or a little salt on the mole of the head for headache. Her sovereign remedy for rheumatism is "'nint de j'ints wid a little kerosene oil an' put some mullen leaves on it." "A good dost of turpentine is good for mos' anything de matter wid you." A coin with a hole in it, usually a dime, tied around the ankle will keep you from getting "pizen." Furthermore, this same treatment warns against the ill effects of getting "conju'ed." "Iffen you gits conju'ed, de dime turn black, an' you kin go to de conju' doctor an' git de conju' took off."

"Is you got to go, Missy? Come back agin. I's allus proud to see you," Aunt Tildy called after me from the edge of the porch.

Mandy McCullough Cosby

Interview with Mandy McCullough Cosby
—Margaret Fowler, Fruithurst, Alabama

THEY CALLED US MCCULLOUGH'S FREE NIGGERS

Mandy McCullough Cosby puffed reflectively at her mellowed corncob pipe and began her story:

"My Massa, Bryant McCullough, was a Chambers county man. He had so many slaves I can't tell you de numbah. He didn't know hisself how many he had. I is now ninety-five years old an' what I remembers mos' is de way de chillun roll aroun' in de big nurses room." Mandy lives at 1508-Pine Street, Anniston, Alabama. She was cutting collards for dinner and left her dishpan and butcher knife to receive her caller.

"Mist' McCullough, he raised niggahs to sell—an' the little black chillen play aroun' until 'bout sundown, dey is give dey supper. A long trough out in a cool place in the bak yard is filled wif good, cold buttermilk an' cornbread crumbed in, an' dey each is give a spoon, an' dey eats dey fill. Den dey is ready fo' bed. Some of dem jes' fall ovah on de groun', asleep, and is picked up, and put on dey pallet in de big chillens room. Dey was old woman called de nurse, look after 'em. Dey git good care fo' de master expects dey will bring good money.

"Ol' Miss, she don't lak to see dem sold, an' she cry ever' time, she so tender-hearted. But Mist' McCullough is jes' lak mens is today. He jes' laugh an' go on.

"But he was good to his black folks. Folks called us 'McCullough's free niggers.' Wasn't much whippin' went on 'roun' our plantation, but on some places close to us, they whipped until blood run down. Some places they even mixed salt an' pepper in water an' bathed 'em with it. The salt water'd heal, but when the pepper got in there, it burned lak fire, an' they'd as well get on to work quick, cause they can't be still nohow.

"One woman, on a plantation not so far from us, was expectin', an' they tied her up under a hack-a-berry tree, an' whipped her until she died. Mos' any time at night ef you go 'roun' that tree, you could hear that baby cry. I 'spect you could hear it yet.

"Everybody said that was murder, an' that something ought to be done
about it, but nothin' ever was.

"Mist' McCullough always give his folks plenty of sumpin' t'eat an' then
he say, 'I's lookin' for plenty uv work.' 'Niggahs fat an' greasy can't do
nothin' but work.

"My mother was a loomer. She didn't do nothin' but weave. We all had
reg'lar stints of spinnin' to do, when we come from the fiel'. We set down
an' eat a good supper, an' ever'night until ten o'clock we spin cuts of
cotton, an' reel the tread, an' nex' day, the rolls is carded an' packed in a
basket to be wove.

"Spinnin' wheels was in every cabin. Dere was so many of us to be tuk
care of, it took lots of spinnin'."

Cheney Cross

Interview with Cheney Cross
—Annie D. Dean

GITTIN' MY PENSION

From all accounts, Aunt Cheney Cross must be quite ninety years old. "In jewin' de war," she says, "I had done long pass my thirteenth birthday." Today Aunt Cheney is a true reflection of slavery days and the Southern mammy.

Away from highways and automobiles, she lives several miles from Evergreen on a small farm in the piney woods with her "baby boy."

Talk with Aunt Cheney reveals that Evergreen's city marshall, Harry L. Riley, "put out to hope" this old family servant who had "tended" to his father, George Riley; his mother, "Miss Narciss," and "Miss Lizzible," his sister. She also helped bring his own "chillun" into the world.

Aunt Cheney had promised Mr. Riley that she would come in town on a certain Saturday morning in May, 1937, and would bring a letter from her young "mistis" for me to read.

It was past noon on that particular Saturday when she came up the back steps, a little out of breath, but smiling. "Lawd, honey," she said, "here 'tis pas' dinner time an' I'se jes' makin' my arrivement here. No'm, I don't wants no dinner, thank you jes' de same. Whut makes me so late here now, I stopped by Miss Ella Northcutt's. She's my folks too, you know, an' she done made me eat all I kin hole! No'm, honey, I can't eat no cabbage. Me an' cabbage never is set horses together much, but I will thank you for the ice tea."

Settling herself down in a low chair, she sighed and began taking off her shoes. "Honey, you don't mind ef I resses my feets does you? My white folks is sp'ilin' me here today. I'll be lookin' for it tomorrrow, too, an' I won't be gittin' it." Her black eyes twinkled in her shiny, old, wrinkled face as she talked on.

"I tole Mr. Harry I'se comin'. An' here I is! How'd I come? I come on Mack and Charlie, dat's how! Yes, ma'am! Dese two boys here, dey brung me." Pushing her feet out for inspection, she leaned forward, smiling and pleased. "Dese here foots, dey's Mack an' Charlie. Dey's my whole pennunce for gittin' about. Don't you worry none. Mr. Harry he'll git be back home 'gainst dark come on.

"Lawd, honey, I don't want to know no better folks'n Mr. Harry an' Miss Emma. I follow dem good folks clean up to Muscle Show! Yessum, I sho' did. At fust, I tole'm I couldn't go nohow. But dey pull down on me so hard, look lack I couldn't he'p myself.

"I stayed on up dere at Muscle Show twell I got so homesick to see my baby boy I couldn't stan' it no mo'. Now, cose, my baby boy he was den de father of his own, a boy an' a girl, but to me dat boy is still jes' my baby, an' I had to come on home."

Aunt Cheney's little, old body shook with laughter as she leaned back and said: "Yes, ma'am! I ain't been home no time atall neither, 'twell here come Mr. Harry back to Evergreen wid his own self. Yes, Lawd! I kin see'm now, comin' up de big hardwood road, his haid raired back, asmokin' a sugarette lack he's a millinery! Lawd, Lawd! Me nor Mr. Harry neither one ain't never gona be contentious nowheres but right here. An' dat's de Gawd's trufe!

"Iffen Mr. Harry hadn't come on back here, I never woulda seed no pension. Dat's de Gawd's trufe, too. Nobody here didn't know my eggzack age, cause dis wasn't my originally home. All dem whut did know close onto my age done died out an' I knows it. So when Mr. Harry put out to hope me, I says in my heart 'Thank Gawd!'

"I tole Mr. Harry dat iffen anybody in de world knowed my age, it was my young mistis, an' I didn't know eggzackly where she at, but her papa was Captain Purifire (Purifoy). Back yonder he was de madistra of our town, an' he had all of dem lawin' books. I figgered dat my birthright would be down in one of dem books. I knowed in reason dat my mistis still got dem books wid her, 'cause dey ain't been no burnin's dat I done heard about. I knowed, too, dat Mr. Harry was gona fine out where she at.

"I 'members Captain Purifire jes' lack a book. I does dat! Now, cose, when he come on in home from de war he didn't 'zackly favor hisse'f den, 'cause when I seed him comin' roun' de house he look so ragged an' ornery I tuck him for de ole Bad Man hisse'f. I tuck out behind de smoke house, an' when I got a good look at him th'ew a crack it look lack I could recognize his favor, but I couldn't call his name to save my life. Lawd, honey! He's a sight! All growed over an' bushy! You couldn't tell iffen he's man or beas'. I kep' on alookin' whilst he's comin' roun' de corner, an' den I heard him say 'Cheney, dat you?' I'se so happy, I jes' melt down."

Aunt Cheney was really living over her past. "You see, it's lack dis," she said: "My fore parents, dey was bought. My Mistis an' my daddy's mistis, too, was Miss Mary Fields, an' my daddy was Henry Fields. Den de Carters bought my daddy from Miss Mary Fields. Well, dey mix up an' down lack dat, twell now my young mistis, what used to be little Frances Purifire, she's married to Mr. Cunningham.

"I was brung up right in de house wid my white folks. Yessum, I slep' on de little trundler bed what pushed up under de big bed, in durinst de day. I watched over dem chillun day an' night. I washed 'em an' fed 'em an' played wid 'em. One of de babies had to take goat's milk. When she cry, my mistis say, 'Cheney, go on an' git dat goat.' Yes Lawd! An' dat goat sho' did talk sweet to dat baby! Jes' lack it was her own. She look at it an' wag her tail so fas' an' say: "Ma-a-a-a!" Den she lay down on de flo' whilst us holes her feets an' let de baby suck de milk. All de time dat goat bees talkin', 'Ma-a-a-a,' twell dat baby got satchified.

"When us chillun got tuck wid any kind of sickness or zeezes, us tuck azzifizzity an' garlit. You know, garlit what smell lack onions. Den we wore some roun' us necks. Dat kep' off flu-anz.

"Dese days it look lack somepin t'eat don't tas'e lack dat we cooked back yonder. De coffee us used had to be fresh groun' ever' day. An' when it commence to bile, I put dese here knees down on de flo' befo' de fire an' stir dat coffee for de longes'. Den my gran'ma she hung dat pot up on dem pot hooks over de fire an' washed de meat an' drap it in. Time she done pick an' overlook de greens an' den wrinched 'em in spring water, de meat was bilin'. Den she take a great big mess of dem fresh turnip greens an' squash 'em down in dat pot. Dey jes' melt down an' go to seasonin'.

"Nex' thing I knowed, here come my mistis, an' she say: 'Now Cheney, I wants some pone bread for dinner.' Dem hick'ry coals in dat fire place was all time ready an' hot. They wouldn't be no finger prints lef' on dat pone when Cheney got th'ew pattin' it out neither. Better not! Look lack dem chillun jes' couldn't git 'nuff of dat hard corn bread.

"Plenty of fancy cookin' went on 'roun' dat fire place, but somehow de pot licker an' pone bread longside wid de fresh buttermilk stirs my mem'ry worse'n anything.

"All dis good eatin' I'se speakin' 'bout tuck place befo' de Yankees raided us. It was den, too, dat my mistis tuck me down to de spring back of de house. Down dere it was a holler tree stump, taller'n you is. She tell me to clam' up to de top of dat holler tree, den she han' me a big heavy bundle, all wropped up an' tied tight. Hit sho' was heavy! Den she say: 'Drap it in, Cheney.' I didn't know den whut she's up to, but dat was de silver an' jew'lry she was hidin'.

"Yes honey, I 'members dat Yankee raid lack it was jes' yistiddy. I'se settin' dere in de loom room, an' Mr. Thad Watts' lil' gal, Louise, she's standin' at the winder. She say: 'O-o-oh! Nannie! Jes' look down yonder!' 'Baby, what is dat?' I says. 'Dem's de Yankees comin'!' 'Gawd hep us!' I says, an' befo' I kin ketch my bref, de place is kivvered. You couldn't stir 'em up wid a stick. Feets sounded lack mutterin' thunder. Dem bayonets stick up lack dey jes' setting on de mouf of dey guns. Dey swords hangin' on dey sides singin' a chune whilst dey walk. A chicken better not pass by. Iffen he do, off come his head!

"When dey pass on by me, dey put' nigh shuck me outa my skin. 'Where's de men's?' dey say an' shake me up. 'Where's de arms?' Dey shake me twell my eye balls loosen up. 'Where's de silver?' Lawd! Was my teefs drappin' out? Dey didn't give me time to ketch my bref. All de time, Miss Mary jes' look 'em in de eye an' say nothin'!

"Dey tuck dem enfield rifles, half as long as dat door, an' bus' in de smoke house winder. Dey jack me up off'n my feet an' drag me up de ladder an' say: 'Git dat meat out.' I kep' on th'owin' out Miss Mary's hams an' sawsidges, twell dey holler 'stop'. I come backin' down dat ladder lack a squirrel, an' I ain't stop backin' twell I retch Miss Mary.

"Yes, Lawd! Dem Yankees loaded up a waggin full of meat an' tuck de whole barrel of 'lasses! Takin' dat 'lasses kilt us chillun! Our mainest 'musement was makin' 'lasses candy. Den us cake walk 'roun' it. Now dat was all gone. Look lack dem sojers had to sharpen dey swords on ever'thing in sight. De big crepe mullen bush by de parlor winder was bloomin' so pink an' pretty, an' dey jes' stood dere an' whack off dem blooms lack folkses heads drappin' on de groun'.

"I seed de sargeant when he run his bayonet clean th'ew Miss Mary's bestest feather bed an' rip it slam open! Wid dat, a win' blowed up an' tuck dem feathers ever' which away for Sunday. You couldn't see where you's at. De sargeant, he jes' th'owed his head back an' laugh fit to kill hisse'f. Den fust thing next, he done suck a feather down his win'pipe! Lawd, honey, dat white man sho' struggled. Dem sojers th'owed water in his face. Dey shuck'm an' beat'm an' roll'm over, an' all de time he's gettin' limberer an' bluerer. Den dey jack him up by his feets an' stan'm on his haid. Den dey pump him up an' down. Den dey shuck'm twell he spit. Den he come to.

"Dey didn't cut no mo' mattrusses. An' dey didn't cut nothin' much up in de parlor, 'cause dat's where de lieutenant an' de sargeant slep'. But dey lef' de nex' day, de whole place was strewed wid mutilation.

"I 'members well back dere in jewin' de war how ever' oncet a month that come 'roun' a big box, longer'n I is an' wider too, was tuck to our sojer boys on de battle fiel'. You never seed de lack of sawsidges dat went in dat box! Wid cake an' chicken an' pies, an' Lawd! de butter all rolled up in corn shucks to keep it fresh. Ever'body from ever'where come to fix dat box an' he'p pile in de stuff. Den you hear 'em say: 'Poor sojers! Put it in here!' Den ever'thing look sorta misty, an' dey haids droop over, lack. Den you see a mother's bres' heave wid her silent prayer.

"Directly atter de surrender, de Ku Kluxes sho' was bad atter de Yankees. Dey do all sorts of things to aggivate 'em. Dey's continual' tyin' grape vines crost de road, to git 'em tangled up an' make 'em trip up an' break dey own necks. Dat was bad too, 'cause dem poor Yankees never s'picioned no better'n dat dem vines jes' blowed down or somepin.

"'Long about den, too, seem lack ha'nts an' spairits was ridin' ever'thing! Dey raided mostly 'roun' de grabeyard. Lawd, honey, I ain't hankerin' atter passin' by no grabeyards. 'Cose, I knows I got to go in dere some day, but dey do make me feel lonesome an' kinder jubus.

"I 'members one night, way back dere, when I'se walkin' down de big road wid Bud, an' he say: 'Look! Didn't you see me give dat road? Dat ha'nt done push me clean outa my place.' Now let me tell you somepin. Iffen you ain't never been dat clost to a ha'nt, you don't know nothin'! I 'lowed he gwine follow me home. When I got dere I shuck mustard seeds down on my flo'. When you sprinkles 'em lack dat he can't git outa dat room twell he done count ever' las' one of dem seed. Well sir, de nex' mawnin' all us could see was somepin lack a lump of jelly layin' dere on de flo' 'mongst dem seeds. Look lack he done counted hisse'f to a pulp.

"After dat night, I puts a big sifter down at my do'. You know ha'nts has to count ever' hole in dat sifter befo' dey can come th'ough. Some folks puts de Bible down dere, too. Den de poor spairit has to read ever' word of dat book befo' he crosses over.

"I reckon 'bout de terriblest thing ever happen to me was dat big lookin' glass. De lookin' glass was all laid out in de top of my trunk, waitin' for my weddin' day. One night I'se standin' by de trunk wid hit wide open. I seed somepin black befo' my eyes an' den a screech owl lit in my winder an' screech right in my face. I'se so scared I sot right down in de middle of dat lookin' glass. Hit bus' in a million pieces! Mamma th'owed up her han's an' holler, 'Git up from dere, gal. You gona have seven years of bad luck. Shoo dat hootin' owl away befo' you dies in your tracks!' Den I swoons off. I feels dem ha'nts gittin' ready to ride me clean down in my grabe. 'Bout den somepin kep' sayin' to me, over an' over: 'Th'ow dem pieces of lookin' glass in runnin' water.' Den hit say: 'Burn your mammy's ole shoe an' de screech owl leave.' Atter I does dat my min' was at res'.

"Soon as my daddy hear 'em firin' off for de Surrender, he put out for de plantation where he fust belong. He lef' me wid my mistis at Pine Flat, but 'twan't long twell he come back to git me an' carry me home wid him. I hates to leave my mistis, an' she didn't want to part from me. She say: 'Stay here wid me, an' I'll give you a school learnin'.' She say to Captain Purifire: 'You go buy my li'l nigger a book. Git one of dem Blue Back Websters,' she say, 'so I kin eddicate her to spell.' Den my daddy say: 'Her mamma tole me not to come home widout her an' she has to go wid me.'

"I never will fergit ridin' behin' my daddy on dat mule way in de night. Us lef' in sich a hurry I didn't git none of my cloze hardly, an' I ain't seed my mistis from dat day to dis!"

Clara Davis

Interview with Clara Davis
—Francois Ludgere Diard

AUNT CLARA DAVIS IS HOMESICK FOR OLD SCENES

"I was bawn in de year 1845, white folks," said Aunt Clara, "on de Mosley plantation in Bellvy jus' nawth of Monroeville. Us had a mighty pretty place back dar. Massa Mosely had near 'bout five hundred acres an' mos' near to one hundred slaves.

"Was Marse Mosely good to us? Lor', honey, how you talk. Co'se he was! He was de bes' white man in de lan'. Us had eve'y thing dat we could hope to eat: turkey, chicken, beef, lamb, poke, vegetables, fruits, aigs, butter, milk ... we jus' had eve'y thing, white folks, eve'ything. Dem was de good ole days. How I longs to be back dar wid my ole folks an' a playin' wid de chilluns down by de creek. 'Tain't nothin' lak it today, nawsuh. When I tell you 'bout it you gwine to wish you was dar too.

"White folks, you can have your automobiles an' paved streets an' electric lights. I don't want 'em. You can have de busses an' street cars an' hot pavements an' high buildin' 'caze I ain't got no use for 'em no way. But I'll tell you what I does want. I wants my ole cotton bed an' de moonlight nights a shinin' through de willow trees an' de cool grass under my feets as I runned aroun' ketchin' lightnin' bugs. I wants to hear de sound of de hounds in de woods atter de 'possum, an' de smell of fresh mowed hay. I wants to feel de sway of de ol' wagon a-goin' down de red, dusty road an' listen to de wheels groanin' as dey rolls along. I wants to sink my teeth into some of dat good ol' ash cake, an' smack de good ol' sorghum offen my mouth. White folks, I wants to see de boats a passin' up an' down de Alabamy ribber an' hear de slaves a singin' at dere work. I wants to see de dawn break over de black ridge an' de twilight settle over de place spreadin' a sort of orange hue over de place. I wants to walk de paths th'ew de woods an' see de rabbits an' watch de birds an' listen to frogs at night. But dey tuk me away f'om dat a long time ago. 'Twern't long befo' I ma'ied an' had chilluns, but don't none of 'em 'tribute to my suppote now. One of 'em was killed in de big war wid Germany and de res' is all scattered out ... eight of 'em. Now I jus' live f'om han' to mouth; here one day, somewhere else de nex'. I guess we's all a-goin' to die iffen dis 'pression don't let us 'lone. Maybe someday I'll git to go home. Dey tells me dat when a pusson crosses dat ribber, de Lawd gives him whut he wants. I done tol' de Lawd I don't want nothin' much ... only my home, white folks. I don't think dat's much to axe for. I supposed he'll sen' me back dar. I been a-waitin' for him to call."

Ella Dilliard

Personal interview with Ella Dilliard
756 Canal Street, Mobile, Alabama
—Ila B. Prine

ELLA'S WHITE HEN IS HEAPS OF COMPANY

Ella Dilliard, an old Negro woman who lives at 756 Canal Street, Mobile, says she was a small girl during slavery time, and does not know the hardships of it, because she was owned by good people. Her mother's name was Mary Norris, owned by Mrs. Calvin Norris, who lived in Selma, Ala., but had a homestead in Mobile. Her father belonged to people by the name of Childress, and his name was Green Childress. She doesn't remember much about him because his white people took him to Texas.

Ella said that her mother was her madame's hairdresser, and that Mrs. Norris had her mother taught in Mobile. So Ella's life was very easy, as she stayed around the big house with her mother, although her grandmother, Penny Anne Norris, cared for her more than her mother did. One of the things she remembers quite distinctly was her grandmother's cooking on the fireplace, and how she would not allow any one to spit in the fireplace. She said her grandmother made corn-pone and wrapped it in shucks and baked it in ashes.

Ella said she did not know many colored people, since the quarters were quite a ways from the big house, and that the plantation was managed by an overseer. She said the quarters were built in rows with streets between them.

She also remembers the first boat she ever saw that was when she was brought to Mobile after the surrender, and when she saw the boat she said to her mother: "Look at that house sitting on the water."

Ella said that there were three cooks at the big house, their names being Hannah, Judy, and Charlotte, and the gardener's name was Uncle John. Ella also said that one thing that she remembers so well about the kitchen in the big house was a large dishpan, that had a partition in the middle of it, one side you washed the dishes in, and the other side was used for scalding them.

The slaves always had Saturdays to wash their clothes and do things for themselves. Ella, not having lived among Negroes, does not know much about their habits and customs, but she does remember seeing the big white covered wagons that the slaves were carried in to be sold; and remembers hearing talk of the "Pattyrollers." She said when the slaves were sold, they were put on a block, and that the man who were buying would look in their mouths just like they did horses.

Ella said she was born in Greensboro, Alabama, but the plantation where she later lived was on the Alabama river near Selma, Ala. She doesn't know how many acres it comprised, or how many slaves that her master owned. She remembers her madame made her stop calling her mother "mammy," and her father "daddy." She said: "You know, Miss, that the white children now-a-days calls their parents 'mammy and daddy' like the colored people used to. The children now do not respect their parents as they should, and in fact everything is so different the truth done 'be under the table.' You know, miss, I am telling the truth, because the Bible says, 'Woe be unto the one that lies; Judgment is on the land.'

"In those days people had to work to live, and they raised most everything they used, such as cattle, hogs, cotton, and foodstuff. Then the women spun the thread out of the cotton, and wove the cloth."

Ella helped her grandmother at the weaving by picking up the shuttles for her. She said they generally used the cloth as it was woven. The shoes were made on the place and were called red brogans.

As for the churches, the white folks had the brush arbor camp meetings, where the people would go and camp in little cabins for weeks, so they could attend the church. They had newspapers then, Ella said, "but 'course they ain't like you have now, there warn't so many as there is now.

"You asked something, miss, about medicines. I don't remember much about any medicine, because Mr. Calvin Norris was a doctor, and he always treated us when we were sick. There was a Dr. Browder who 'tended the plantation."

Ella is a bright colored, small woman, whose eyes are very keen. She says that a short time ago she had some trouble with her eyes, and she got something from the drug store to bathe them with, but it did not help them. So she caught some pure rain water and "anointed" her eyes with that, and now she can see to thread a needle. Her life has been very colorful in many respects. She recalled as a small child, that, during the war, a minie-ball came through a brick wall of the servant house where they were living, but it fell without harming any of the servants. She said when Wilson's raid was made on Selma, that the Yankee men went through the houses just like dogs, taking whatever they wanted.

"I 'members Mr. Parkman putting two sacks of money down in his big well, and him getting it out with hooks after the Yankees left."

Later when she was brought to Mobile she worked for Judge Oliver Semmes for twenty years. Judge Semmes was the son of Admiral Raphael Semmes, and she said he was a blessed, good man. For the past fourteen years she has been working for the Frank Lyons family of Mobile.

Ella lives in a double tenement house, having one room and a small kitchen. The room is full of old furniture and odd things. On the mantle is a lovely old china pitcher that once was owned by Judge Semmes and which Ella prizes very much. The thing that puzzles Ella most among the modern inventions, she said, are the aeroplanes, and the way ice is made. She said:

"Miss, we never had any ice way back yonder. We had nice, old, open brick wells, and the water was just like ice. We would draw the water and put around the milk and butter in the dairy. It's a mystery to me how they make that ice, but, my goodness! I guess I need not worry my head about things, because I am not here for long. All my family is dead and gone now, and the only companion I have is this here little white hen. Her name is Mary. You see, I bought her last year to kill for Christmas, but I couldn't do it. She is so human; and you ought to see the eggs she lays. I even have a few to sell sometimes. I just keeps Mary in the room at night with me, and she is heaps of company for me."

Rufus Dirt

Interview with Rufus Dirt
—Woodrow Hand, Birmingham, Alabama

RUFUS WOULD TALK A LOT FOR A DIME

Foreword: This Negro, Rufus Dirt, was found on one of Birmingham's busiest streets begging for coins. Because of his inability to read, he was unable to give the number or location of his home. All he knew was "jes' som'ers on Southside, boss."

"I'll drop a dime in your hat uncle if you'll stand here and talk to me for a few minutes."

"Sho' boss, iffen you wants, I'll talk all day fo' dat much money. I'se been here fo' a long time an' I knows plenty to talk 'bout. What does yo' want to know?"

I explained my interest in slavery days and my search for ex-slaves, but he began telling me before I had time to finish. His ability to talk had somehow escaped what his age had done to his hair, which was sparse as well as snowy white. His eyes were a glazy red. One hand and arm seemed to be crippled, but the other waved around in the air as he talked and finally settled on my shoulder.

"Boss, I don' rightly know jes' how old I is. I was a driver (Negro boss of other slaves) during slavery and I reckons I was about twenty sompin'. I don' remember nothin' in particular that caused me to get dat drivin' job, ceptin' hard work, but I knows dat I was proud of it 'cause I didn' have to work so hard no mo'. An' den it sorta' made de other niggers look up to me, an' you knows us niggers, boss. Nothin' makes us happier dan' to strut in front of other niggers. Dere ain't nothin' much to tell about. We jes' moved one crop atter de other till layin' by time come and den we'd start in on de winter work. We done jes' 'bout de same as all de other plantations.

"My massa's name was Digby and we live at Tuscaloosa befo' de war. An' 'bout dat war, white folks. Dem was some scary times. De nigger women was a-feared to breathe out loud come night an' in de day time, dey didn't work much 'cause dey was allus lookin' fo' de Yankees. Dey didn' come by so much 'cause atter de first few times. Dere wa'nt no reason to come by.

Dey had done et up ever'thing and toted off what dey didn' eat. Dey tuk all Massa's stock, burned down de smokehouse atter dey tuk de meat out, an' dey burned de barn, an' we'all think ever' time dat dey goin' to burn de house down, but dey musta forgot to do dat.

"When de war was finally over an' I was free, my family went to Vicksburg, Mississippi where we made a livin' first one way an' den de other. I don't know how long we stayed dere, but I was livin' in Bummin'ham when dere wa'nt nothin' much here a'tall. I watched all de big buildin's 'round here go up and I see'd dem build all de big plants and I'se still watchin', but I still don' know how to tell folks where places is, 'cause I don' know how to read numbers. I goes anywhere I wants to go an' I don't ever get lost, but jes' de same, I can't tell nobody where I am. I don' even know where we is standin' talking like dis right now. An' boss, I ain't beggin' 'cause I'se too lazy to work. I'se worked plenty in my time till I crippled dis arm in de mines and befo' my eyes got so bad," and with a grace and gentleness that may be called a characteristic of his generation, he added, "I hope I'se told you what you wants to know."

He had. I felt well repaid for the dime I had given him. As he walked off down the street, I noticed for the first time the large crowd that had gathered around us. Evidently slave tales carry more interest than this writer realized.

Katherine Eppes

Interview with Katherine Eppes
—Susie R. O'Brien, Uniontown, Alabama

CABINS AS FAR AS YOU COULD SEE

"Ma" Eppes sat on the steps of her weatherbeaten, unpainted little cabin, duplicate of the dozens that make up Rat Row, Negro quarter of Uniontown, and looked down the vista of memory to her childhood when she lived in "where de log cabins stretched as far as you could see in de slave qua'ters."

Despite her eighty-seven years, Katherine Eppes, known to everyone as "Ma," came as spryly to her tiny porch as her rotund body would permit. She smiled broadly at her interviewer and seated herself slowly.

"Sho', honey, I can tell you mo'n anything you want to know 'bout the big fight, 'ca'se I been here a long time," she began her story. "Dey ain't many lef' to tell 'bout dem days. My mammy an' pappy was Peter an' Emma Lines an' us all belonged to Marsa Frank and Miss Sarah Lines. I was born on dey plantation five miles below Faunsdale 'bout 1850 so dey tells me.

"I is right ol' but thank Gawd I still got my teefies an' my ha'r lef'." Proudly the old woman unwrapped her "head rag" to display a thick mop, woolly white but neatly parted into squares. Dozens of little plaits, wrapped with yards of twine, just as her hair had been dressed in the slave quarters before the War, adorned her head. She sat with uncovered head unblinking in the bright June sunshine, as she took up the tale of her health. "I sees pretty good, too, but I's so hebby I ain't able to toe myse'f 'roun' as pert as I useter.

"It was diff'rent back in dem days when I belonged to rich white folks. Dey had plenty of niggers an' dey was log cabins in de quarters jes' as far as your eyes could see. Marsa Frank an' Miss Sarah was good to de black folks, too. Dey son, young marsa Frank, fit in de big war. Atter de war was over I stayed on de Lines' place 'twell atter I ma'ied, an' Ol' Miss gin me my weddin' dress an' a long veil down to my foots.

"When us was chillun in de quarters we did a mighty lot of playin'. Us useta play 'Sail away Rauley' a whole lot. Us would hol' han's an' go 'roun' in a ring, gittin' faster an' faster an' dem what fell down was outa de game.

"My mammy wukked in de Big House, aspinnin' an' anussin' de white chillun. All of dem called her 'mammy.' Ah 'members one thing jes' lack it was yestiddy. Miss Sarah went to 'Mospolis (Demopolis) to visit wid her sister, an' whilst she were gone de oberseer, what go by de name of Allen, whupped my Mammy crost her back 'twell de blood runned out.

"When Miss Sarah comed back an' foun' it out, she was de maddes white lady I eber seed. She sont for de oberseer, an' she say: 'Allen, what you mean by whupping Mammy? You know I don't allow you to tech my house servants.' She jerk her dress down an' stan' dere lookin' like a sojer wid her white shoulders shinin' lack a snow bank, an' she say: 'I 'druther see dem marks on my own shoulders dan to see 'em on Mammy's. Dey wouldn't hurt me no wuss.' Den she say: 'Allen, teck your fambly an' git offen my place. Don't you let sundown ketch you here. 'So he lef'. He wasn't nothin' but white trash nohow."

"Ma" Eppes sat silent for a time as she recalled the vision of Miss Sarah standing straight and regal in her dismissal of the overseer. Finally she turned with an abrupt change of subject.

"Honey, is you a Christian?" she asked earnestly. "I hopes you is, ca'se you is too fine lookin' for to go to Hell. I b'longs to de Baptis' Church, an' dey calls me Ma Eppes 'ca'se I's de mother of de church. I loves to sing de gospel Hymns."

She began to sing in a high, cracked voice, her body swaying with the rhythm. The song rose until her neighbors had gathered to form quite an audience. With much moaning between every line, she sang:

"I am a sojer of de Cross,
A follerer of de Lam'.
I'm not afeard to own His name,
Nor to 'fen' His cause."

(Chorus)

"I wan' you to come,

I wan' you to come,
I wan' you to come
An' be saved."

She was still singing as I left her, the neighbors joining in the choruses. Suppers would be late in the row of weatherbeaten cabins, because the spirit of song was on the gathering.

Reuben Fitzpatrick

Interview with Reuben Fitzpatrick
—[HW: *Mabel Farrior, Montgomery, Alabama]*

A HORN FOR A HEADACHE

Reuben Fitzpatrick, of Eugene Street, Montgomery, was born Jan. 9, 1854, (83 years old). He says:

"My Marster was Mister Gholson frum Bullock county. He had lots uv slaves 'cause he was a rich man. I was jes' a boy ten years ole an' he was a squire dat tried cases, so he rode all over de country to dif'funt places. I rode wid him to hole his horse. He wore a high top black hat and had a buggy wid a top dat let back. When we went we was gone a long time an' when night come he would fix it fer me to sleep wid some uv de niggers in de quarters where we stopped. I sho' lacked to go 'bout wid him.

"My mother was de cook. She had rule over all the cookin'. She spinned thread an' reeled it off too.

"When de Yankees come through de country I seed 'em all runnin' so I thought it was jedgment day an' I runned an' hid under de chimney an' stayed dere 'tel night. Dey didn't tarry long, but dey drove de horses right up on de piazza, and throwed ever' thing out de houses, eben knocked down de smoke 'ouse doors. Dat's de trufe'.

"One time I was taken to the slave market and I was screwed on the block and Mr. Martin bought me and my Mamma. The man that was selling us would holler, "Who'll bid? Who'll bid?" We was supposed to be spry and fidgety so as to make the men want to buy us. My fust Marster was Wash Jones. He wan't good to us. He would hit us wid his cane jes' as if it had been a switch. Ben Jones didn't like the way Marse Wash treated us niggers. He bought us for his son.

"We didn't have no doctors much in dem days, but us had a horn us use when we got sick. If us had the headache that horn would go right over the spot and it wouldn't be no time 'fore the pain'd be gone. We'd use that horn anytime we was ailing an' it'd sho' do the work. I used to have the horn but I don't know jes' where it is now."

Heywood Ford

Interview with Heywood Ford
—Susie R. O'Brien, Uniontown, Alabama

HEYWOOD FORD TELLS A STORY

"White folks," said Heywood Ford, "I'se gonna tell you a story 'bout a mean oberseer an' whut happened to him durin' de slabery days. It all commenced when a nigger named Jake Williams got a whuppin' for stayin' out atter de time on his pass done gib out. All de niggers on de place hated de oberseer wuss dan pizen, 'caze he was so mean an' useta try to think up things to whup us for.

"One mornin' de slaves was lined up ready to eat dere breakfas' an' Jake Williams was a pettin' his ole red-bone houn'. 'Bout dat time de oberseer come up an' seed Jake a pettin' his houn' an' he say: 'Nigger you ain't got time to be a-foolin' 'long dat dog. Now make him git.' Jake tried to make de dog go home, but de dog didn't want to leave Jake. Den de oberseer pick up a rock an' slam de dog in de back. De dog he den went a-howlin' off.

"Dat night Jake he come to my cabin an' he say to me: 'Heywood, I is gonna run away to a free State. I ain't a-gonna put up wid dis treatment no longer. I can't stand much mo'. I gibs him my han' an' I say: 'Jake, I hopes you gits dere. Maybe I'll see you ag'in sometime.'

"'Heywood,' he says, 'I wish you'd look atter my houn', Belle. Feed her an' keep her de bes' you kin. She a mighty good possum an' coon dog. I hates to part wid her, but I knows dat you is de bes' pusson I could leave her wid.' An' wid dat Jake slip out de do' an' I seed him a-walkin' toward de swamp down de long furrows of cawn.

"It didn't take dat oberseer long to fin' out dat Jake done run away, an', when he did, he got out de blood houn's an' started off atter him. It warn't long afore Jake heered dem houn's a-howlin' in de distance. Jake he was too tired to go any further. He circled 'roun' an' doubled on his tracks so as to confuse de houn's an' den he clumb a tree. T'warn't long afore he seed de light of de oberseer comin' th'ough de woods and de dogs was a-gittin' closer an' closer. Finally dey smelled de tree dat Jake was in an' dey started barkin' 'roun' it. De oberseer lif' his lighted pine knot in de air so's he could see Jake. He say: 'Nigger, come on down fum dere. You done wasted 'nuff of our time.' But Jake, he neber move nor make a sound an' all de time de dogs keppa howlin' an' de oberseer keppa swearin'. 'Come on down,' he say ag'in; 'iffen you don't I'se comin' up an' knock you outen de tree wid a stick.' Jake still he neber moved an' de oberseer den began to climb de tree. When he got where he could almos' reach Jake he swung dat stick an' it come down on Jake's leg an' hurt him tur'ble. Jake, he raised his foot an' kicked de oberseer raght in de mouf, an' dat white man went a tumblin' to de groun'. When he hit de earth dem houn's pounced on him. Jake he den lowered hisself to de bottom limbs so's he could see what had happened. He saw de dogs a-tearin' at de man an' he holla: 'Hol' 'im, Belle! Hol' 'im, gal!' De leader of dat pack of houn's, white folks, warn't no blood houn'. She was a plain old red-bone possum an' coon dog, an' de res' done jus' lak she done, tearin' at de oberseer's th'oat. All de while, Jake he a-hollerin' fum de tree fer dem dogs to git 'im. 'Twarn't long afore dem dogs to' dat man all to pieces. He died raght under dat maple tree dat he run Jake up. Jake he an' dat coon houn' struck off through de woods. De res' of de pack come home.

"I seed Jake atter us niggers was freed. Dat's how come I knowed all 'bout it. It musta been six years atter dey killed de oberseer. It was in Kentucky dat I run across Jake. He was a-sittin' on some steps of a nigger cabin. A houn' dog was a-sittin' at his side. I tells him how glad I is to see him, an' den I look at de dog. 'Dat ain't Belle,' I says. 'Naw,' Jake answers, 'Dis her puppy.' Den he tol' me de whole story. I always did want to know what happen to 'em."

Georgia

Interview with Georgia
—Gertha Couric

DEY PLANTED DE SILVER IN DE FIEL'

"No, honey, I neber seed my mammy. She died when I was bawn, an' my Mistis Mary Mitchell raised me in de Big House. I was named a'ter her sister, Miss Georgia. I slep' in her room an I was a house nigger all my days. I neber went to a nigger chu'ch 'tell I was grown an' ma'd, didn' sociate wid niggers 'cause I was a nu'smaid. I raised Miss Molly, her las' baby.

"I was bawn at 'Elmoreland', Massa Americus Mitchell's place, mor'n ninety yeahs ago, an' a'ter freedom I stayed dah 'tel ole Massa died an' my Mistis moved to Eufaula to live wid her son, Mahs Merry.

"'Bout all I know of de wawh is when dey said—'de Yankees is comin', de Yankees is comin'.'

"Us sho' was skeerd, an' dere'd be some fas' doin's about de place. All de cattle an' hawgs an hosses we driv' to de swamp on de nawth creek, an' de feather beds down dere too an' hid 'em in de brush an' leaves. My Mistis tied her trinkets in sacks an' put 'em in outlandish places lak de hen-house an de hay lof'. An' de silver, dey planted in de fiel."

Fannie Gibson

Interview with Fannie Gibson
—J.R. Jones, Columbus, Georgia

Fannie Gibson was born the slave property of Mr. Benajer Goff, a planter of near Roanoke, Alabama. She says that during her girlhood she "piddled in de fiels an hepped in de kitchen o' de big house."

She has very pleasant memories of slave days, and "wishes to God dat she was as comforbly (comfortably) fixed now as she was den."

Her ante-bellum owner she pictures as a very humane, Christian gentleman—a man that took great interest in the material and spiritual welfare of his slaves.

Two hymns, sung by 'Aunt' Fannie for her interviewer, are appended.

Going Home To Live With The Lord.

Goin' home soon in de mornin',
Goin' home soon in de mornin',
I's goin' home to live with de Lord.

In de mornin' so soon,
In de mornin' so soon,
I's goin' home to live with de Lord.

I's goin' home to live with de Lord,
I's goin' home to live with de Lord,
I's goin' home soon in de mornin'.

O, de Lord is a-waitin' for me,
O, de Lord is a-waitin' for me,
I's goin' home soon in de mornin'.

Where Were You When You Found The Lord?

My brother, where were you,
My brother, where were you,
My brother, where were you,

When you found the Lord?

I was low down in the valley,
I was low down in the valley,
I was low down in the valley,
When I first found the Lord.

My sister, where were you,
My sister, where were you,
My sister, where were you,
When you found the Lord?

I was low down in the valley,
I was low down in the valley,
I was low down in the valley,
When I first found the Lord.

This song can be extended indefinitely by addressing the question to
various members of one's family, and to friends.

Frank Gill

Personal interview with Frank Gill
708 South Hamilton Street, Mobile, Alabama
—Ila B. Prine, Mobile, Alabama

A SLAVE BOY ESCAPES WHIPPING BY PULLING TAIL OF FROCK COAT

A low, stout, sleek headed Negro man, sat in an old rocking chair in an end room of a long row of rooms of a tenement house at 708 South Hamilton Street, Mobile, Alabama. This old darkey said, when asked by the writer if he lived during slavery times: "I not only lived durin' slavery times, but I was here before a gun was fired, an' b'fore Lincoln was elected. I tells you, Miss, de fust time I 'members anything—a tale of any kind. I was livin' in Vicksburg, Lee County, Mississippi, an' mah maw an' paw's names was Amelia Williams an' Hiram Gill. I couldn't tells you whar dey war from, dough. But I does know dat Mista Arthur an' George Foster owned us, up 'til I war a big boy. De way it was, dere mother, Ol' Missy, was a widow, an' her had dese two boys, an' she had money, I tells you she had barrels ob money; so when de two boys got old enough she divide de slaves, an' property 'tween 'em. Me an' mah maw fell to Arthur Foster, and sum ob our kindred fell to George Foster. Mister George was a Captain in de army an' was killed near Vicksburg.

"De Ol' Missy's place shore was big, I couldn't say how many acres dere was, but hit run four or five miles, an' she owned hundreds ob slaves. She had lots ob log cabin quarters, whut had de cracks daubed wid mud, an' den ceiled wid boards. I'se tellin' you dey was twice as warm as de houses we lib in now. Dey had chimbleys built ob mud an' sticks, an' had big wide, fireplaces, dat we cooked on, an' de beds was homemade, but Lor' dey was heaps stronger dan dey is now, in dese times. Dem beds was morticed together.

"As I said b'fore I was a boy between fourteen or fifteen years old b'fore de slaves was divided, an' when I was on de Ol' Missy's place, I stayed aroun' de house, an' wait on dem, an' 'tend de horses. Anudder thing I had to do, dey would send me for the mail. I had to go twelve miles atter hit an' I couldn't read or write, but I could bring everybody's mail to dem jes' right. I knowed I had better git hit right. You see I could kinder figure, so I could make out by de numbers.

"Ol' Missy an' Mister Arthur both was good to me an' all de slaves, dey 'low de slaves to make dere own patch ob cotton, an' raise chickens, an' he would sell hit for dem. Cotton was de main crop, in dem days, hit would sell as high as twenty-five cents a pound. 'Course dey raises corn, pears, an' other things on de plantation, too, but dey made de cotton. Master Jesus! dey sumtimes made from fifty to one hundred an' fifty bales.

"I 'members how all de women had looms, both black and white, weavin' cloth for de clothes; an' den dey raised sheep to git de wool to make dem gray uniforms. Lord, at sheep shearing time! hit was big times. Let me tell you, Miss, dem uniforms was made out ob all wool, too, but I cain't 'member whut dey used to dye 'em gray, but I 'members dey dyed wid red oak bark, walnut bark, an' also a brush whut growed down on the branch, also dey used de laurel leaves to dye yellow, as well as clay. Dey so't de dye wid salt, an' hit really stayed in.

"Let me tell you, dey really fed us slaves good, up 'til such a length o' time atter de war broke out, den food began to git scarce.

"You see de Government taxed 'em, an' dey had to gib so much to feed de soldiers. Even den us had a good time, I 'members how de li'l chillun played ball, and marbles, 'specially marbles, hit was our big game. Even atter night dey had a big light out in de backyard, an' us would play. Sometimes us would hunt at night, and well I 'members one Sat'day night I went huntin' wid mah uncle, an' didn't git in 'til daylight nex' mawning, an' I was sleepy an' didn't git de shoes all cleaned before church time. So ol' Marsar called me an' tuk me to de carriage house to gib me a whippin'. Ol' Marser's boy was about de same age as me an' he beg his paw not to whip me, an' I was beggin', too, but he carried me on, an' when we got in de carriage house, Ol' Marser had to climb up on de side wall to git de whip, an' he had on one ob dos long tailed coats, an' hit left dem tails hangin' down, so I jes' grabbed hold ob dem, an' made him fall, an' den I run to de Ol' Missy's room, 'ca'se I knowed when I got in dere, dat Ol' Marser would neber hit me.

"De Ol' Missy got up out ob de bed an' wouldn't let Ol' Marster whip me, an' she got so mad dat she tol' him dat she warn't going to church wid him dat morning, an' dat lack to kill de Ol' Marster, 'ca'se he shore loved an' was proud ob Ol' Missy. She was a beautiful woman. Dat ended de whippin', an' dat's de only time I 'members him tryin' to whip me.

"Ol' Missy didn't 'low dem to whip de women either, an' dey wouldn't 'low de women to roll logs either. But dey did work dem in de fiel's. 'Course dey kept de young women wid babies 'roun' de house, an' dey eat de same grub as de white folks eat.

"Talking 'bout log rollin', dem was great times, 'ca'se if some ob de neighborin' plantations wanted to get up a house, dey would invite all de slaves, men and women, to come wid dere masters. De women would help wid de cookin' an' you may be shore dey had something to cook. Dey would kill a cow, or three or four hogs, and den hab peas, cabbage, an' everything lack grows on de farm. An' if dere was any meat or food lef' dey would gib dat to de slaves to take home, an' jes' b'fore dark de o'seer or Ol' Marster would gib de slaves all de whiskey dey wanted to drink. Sometimes atter de days work, dey would hab a frolic, such as dancin', an' ol' time games.

"Dey would hab dese same kind ob gatherin's at cornshucking time, an' cotton pickin' time, but dere warn't so much foolishness at cotton pickin' time, 'ca'se dey didn't call one anudder den, 'ceptin' when de cotton got so far ahead ob dem, an' was 'bout to set in fer a wet spell, or rainy season.

"You axed me 'bout de patty-rollers? You see de City policemen walkin' his beat? Well, dat's de way de patty-rollin' was, only each county had dere patty-rollers, an' dey had to serve three months at a time, den dey was turned loose. And if dey cotch you out widout a pass, dey would gib you thirty-nine lashes, 'ca'se dat was de law. De patty-rollers knowed nearly all de slaves, an' it wurn't very often dey ever beat 'em.

"You know folks was jes' de same den as dey is now, both black, and white. Some folks you could neighbor wid den, jes' lack you can now, an' dere was good folks den, jes' de same as dey is now.

"Christmas time was de bes' ob all, 'ca'se us allus had a big dinner, an' de Ol' Marster gib de women calico dresses an' shoes, an' de men shoes an' hats, an' would gib us flour, an' sugar, molasses, an' would buy beer, whiskey an' wine.

"De Ol' Marster tuk good keer ob us too, when any ob us got sick he send for de doctor, den when dey order de medicine to be giben at night, he'd see dat us got hit. But nowadays if you git sick, you hab to git de Doctor, an' den pay him yo' se'f. Den de Ol' Marster had to find clothes an' shoes for us, but now us has to scuffle an' git dem de bes' way us can.

"You know, Miss, I'se been here a long time, I eben 'members Jefferson Davis. I'se seen him many a time. He had a home 'tween here (Mobile) an' New Orleans, an' you knows he fust tuk his seat in Montgomery, an' den moved to Richmond, Virginny.

"I 'members, too, how I useta to think dat de Baptist was de only religion. You see John de Baptist come here baptizing, an' ever'body had to offer up sacrifices, a goat or a sheep or sumpin', jes' lack de man who was going to offer up his son for a sacrifice. But you knows, Jesus come an' changed all dat. De folks in dem times didn't hab nobody to worship; an' den one come, who said, 'Father, hand me a body, and I'll die for dem,' Dat's Christ, an' he was baptized, an' God gib Jesus dis whole world. So I believed, dat was de only religion.

"I 'members how us would hab big baptizings an' shout. Us allus went to church in de white folks church, dey had church in de mornings, us had ours in de afternoons. Us would hab to hab a pass, dough, 'ca'se de church was eight miles away from de plantation.

"Dere was plenty old songs us useta to sing, but I can't 'member 'em. Dere is dis one dat goes—

Wonderful Peter,
Wonderful Paul,
Wonderful Silas,
Who for to make a
Mah heart rejoice.

On Good Shepherds, feed a' mah sheep.
Don't you hear de young lambs a bleatin'?
Don't you hear de young lambs a bleatin'?
Don't you hear de young lambs a bleatin'?
Oh! Good shepherds feed a' mah sheep."

Jim Gillard

Interview with Jim Gillard
—Preston Klein, Opelika, Alabama

SOLD AT THREE MONTHS FOR $350

Jim Gillard was eleven years old when the War between the States began. Thus, the memories of the conflict are fresh; with the retreat from Rome, Ga., to Salem, Ala., as a refugee, transcending the others.

Jim was born on a plantation at Pendleton, S.C., and was sold for $350 when he was only three months old. He was one of eight children belonging to James and Hannah Gillard.

"Atter bein' sold, I fust lived 'bout three miles from Rome, Ga.," Jim recalled. "Den, when de Yankees come into Georgy us refugeed fust to Atlanta, den to Columbus an' later to Salem. Us was at Salem when de war ended."

Jim remembers catching partridges as a boy, taking them to the train and selling them to Charlie Crowder for ten cents each.

"Game was plentiful in dem days," he said, "an' I never had any trouble catchin' dem birds.

"No'm, our houses wasn't nothin' to brag about. Dey was built of hewn logs an' had slab floors, havin' two rooms an' a shed cook room. Us beds was lak tables, wid four legs nailed on to de sides an' den corded over de top wid ropes dat was tightened wid a big key. Us had shuck mattresses to sleep on.

"Us cooked on a great big fireplace. I 'members dat dere was plenty of meat in de winter, 'ca'se Ol' Marster used to kill as many as thirty hogs at a time. Us had meat an' bread an' home-made light bread an' de white folks was mighty kind. I 'members us was carried to Sunday School every Sunday at 3 o'clock in de evenin'. Ol' Mistus'd teach us de lesson. De white chilluns had dere Sunday School at 9 o'clock in de mornin.'

"I allus went to Sunday School, but on de week days us little niggers would slip off an' go huntin' when we could."

Jim recalls that "de little niggers" ate from tin plates on the plantation; but declared he didn't mind that because the food was always good.

"Yes'm, us had purty good clothes. Dey was dyed brown wid walnut leaves an' hazelnut bush, an' on Sunday us had striped gingham pants an' shoes. My father was de shoemaker an' had a gov'mint tan yard whar he would make ol' hard brogans fer $8 a pair.

"My marster an' Mistus was Steven an' 'Lizbeth Wilson. Dey fust lived in a big log house, but den moved into a planked house. Dey had nine chillun; Ann, Steven, William, Liza, Humie, Eddie, Laura, Mary an' Lizzie.

"I 'members lots 'bout Mistus 'Lizabeth, 'ca'se she useter read de Bible to us niggers. She would talk to us 'bout de Good Book an' have prayer meetin' wid us.

"My dad useter look atter de fiel' hands. No'm, he war'nt no overseer, but Ol' Marster allus had confidence in him.

"I 'members dat when dey would be a funeral, us'd sing; marchin' befo' de body 'fore us'd get to de grave an' singin', 'Hark come de tune a doleful sound, my years a tender cry; a livin' man come view de ground whar you may shortly lie.'

"Us frolics on Sattidy night was fine an' us'd dance 'twel mos' day. Marster's brother would fiddle for us, an' at Christmas time us would have six days to frolic. Us also had a big time at de cornshuckin's, an' us'd whoop an' holler an' sing mos' all night. De big niggers had plenty of liquor de boss give 'um. High tables was filled up wid corn an' de niggers would shuck 'twel it was all done.

"My aunt married up at de big house an' dey give her a big dance. Dey had de fiddle and had a great big time. Dey jes' jumped over de broom to marry, so atter slavery dey had to git married agin.

"I acted as houseboy in slavery times. An' all de little niggers did have lots of fun.

"When de slaves got ailin', I 'members dat Marster had Dr. Word an' Dr. Dunwoody to come to see us.

"I 'members, too, how de Yankees come to Spring Villa, 'bout eight miles from Opelika, an' said to some mens, 'Halt'. De mens wouldn't stop so de Yankees throwed dey guns on dem. Two white ladies threw a white flag an' dey wouldn't shoot, but dey carried Mr. John Edwards to Spring Villa an' made a cross on his wrist; den turned him loose 'ca'se his wife was rale sick.

"When de Yankees come, us niggers buried a cigar box wid de jewelry in it under a certain pine tree 'twel dey went on.

"Atter de big war, I married Jane Davis fust time; den Carrie Cooper. Us had two chillun an' one gran' chile, Emanuel Trotter, ten year' old.

"Yassu'm, Mr. Abraham Lincoln died a warrior for dis country. I b'longs to de church, 'ca'se if a man dies outter de Ark he is not saved, an' I wants to be saved."

Mary Ella Grandberry

Interview with Mary Ella Grandberry
—Levi D. Shelby, Jr., Tuscumbia, Alabama

TODAY'S FOLKS DON'T KNOW NOTHIN'

Life as a child is not clear in the ninety-year old memory of Mary Ella Grandberry, who lives in Sheffield, but she remembers that she did not have time to play as do children of today.

"I don't know jes' how old I is," Mary Ella said, "but I knows dat I'm some'ers nigh ninety yars ol'. I was borned in Barton, Alabama. My father an' mother come from Richmond, Virginny. My mammy was name Margaret Keller an' my pappy was Adam Keller. My five sisters was Martha, Sarah, Harriet, Emma an' Rosanna, an' my three brothers was Peter, Adam, Jr., an' William.

"Us all live in a li'l two-room log cabin jes' off the Big House. Life wan't ver' much for us, 'caze we had to work an' slave all de time. Massa Jim's house was a little ol' frame buildin' lack a ord'nary house is now. He was a single man an' didn't hab so terr'ble much, it seem. He had a whole lot, too, but jes' to look at him you'd thank he was a po' white man. Dere was a lot o' cabins for de slaves, but dey wasn't fitten for nobody to lib in. We jes' had to put up wid 'em.

"I don' 'member much about when I was a chil'. I disremembers ever playin' lack chilluns do today. Ever since I kin 'member I had a water bucket on my arm totin' water to de han's. Iffen I wan't doin' dat, I was choppin' cotton. Chilluns nowadays sees a good time to w'at we did den. Ever' mornin' jes' 'bout hip of day de oberseer was 'roun' to see dat we was ready to git to de fiel's. Plenty times us had to go widouten breakfas', 'caze we didn' git up in time to git it 'fo' de man done come to git us on de way to de fiel'. Us wukked 'twell dinner time jes' de same before we got anythang to eat.

"De food we et was fix jes' lack hit is now. My mammy fixed our grub at home. De on'y diffe'nce 'tween den an' now was us didn' git nothin' but common things den. Us didn' know what hit was to git biscuits for breakfas' ever' mornin'. It was cornbread 'twell on Sundays den us'd git fo' biscuits apiece. Us got fatback mos' ever' mornin'. Sometimes us mought

51

git a chicken for dinner on a Sunday or some day lack Chris'mas. It was mighty seldom us gits anythin' lack dat, dough. We lacked possums an' rabbits but dey didn' come twell Winter time when some of de men folks'd run 'crost one in de fiel'. Dey never had no chanst to git out an' hunt none.

"Dere was no sech thang as havin' diffe'nt clo's for winter an' Summer. Us wore de same thang in summertime as in de wintertime. De same was true 'bout shoes. Us wore brogans from one yeah to de yuther.

"My Ol' Massa was a putty good man but nothin' exter. One thang 'bout him, he wouldn' 'low none of de oberseers to whup none of us, lessen he was dar to see hit done. Good thang he was lack dat, too, 'caze he sabed de blacks a many a lick what dey'd got iffen he hadn' been dar. Massa Jim was a bach'lor, an' he ain't never had much truck wid women folks. Iffen he had any chilluns, I never knowed nothin' 'bout 'em.

"De oberseers was terrible hard on us. Dey'd ride up an' down de fiel' an' haste you so twell you near 'bout fell out. Sometimes an' most inginer'ly ever' time you 'hin' de crowd you got a good lickin' wid de bull whup dat de driver had in de saddle wid him. I hearn mammy say dat one day dey whupped po' Leah twell she fall out like she was daid. Den dey rubbed salt an' pepper on de blisters to make 'em burn real good. She was so so' 'twell she couldn' lay on her back nights, an' she jes' couldn' stan' for no clo's to tech back whatsomever.

"Massa Jim had 'bout one of de bigges' plantations in dat section. I guess he had nigh onto a hun'erd blacks on de place. I never knowed 'zackly how many thar was nor how big de place was.

"De folks now'days is allus complainin' 'bout how dey is havin' sech hard times, but dey jes' don' know nothin'. Dey should hab come up when I did an' dey'd see now dey is libin' jes' lack kings an' queens. Dey don' have to git up 'fo' day when hit's so dark you kin jes' see your han's 'fo' your eyes. Dey don' know what it's lack to have to keep up wid de leader. You know dey was allus somebody what could wuk faster dan de res' of de folks an' dis fellow was allus de leader, an' ever'body else was s'pose to keep up wid him or her whatsomever hit was. Iffen you didn' keep up wid de leader you got a good thrashin' when you gits home at night. Hit was allus good dark when de han's got in from de fiel'. Co'se iffen dar was a lady what had a baby at home, she could leave jes' a little 'fo' de sun sot.

"Younguns now'days don' know what it is to be punish'; dey thank iffen dey gits a li'l whuppin' from dey mammy now dat dey is punish' terrible. Dey should of had to follow de leader for one day an' see how dey'd be punish' iffen dey gits too far behin'. De bigges' thang dat us was punish' for was not keepin' up. Dey'd whup us iffen we was caught talkin' 'bout de free states, too. Iffen you wan't whupped, you was put in de 'nigger box' an' fed cornbread what was made widouten salt an' wid plain water. De box was jes' big 'nough for you to stan' up in, but hit had air holes in hit to keep you from suffocatin'. Dere was plenty turnin' 'roun' room in hit to 'low you to change your position ever' oncet in a while. Iffen you had done a bigger 'nough thang you was kep' in de 'nigger box' for months at de time, an' when you got out you was nothin' but skin an' bones an' scurcely able to walk.

"Half de time a slave didn' know dat he was sol' 'twell de massa'd call him to de Big House an' tell him he had a new massa from den on. Ever' time dat one was sol' de res' of 'em'd say, 'I hopes nex' time'll be me.' Dey thought you'd git a chanst to run away to de free states. I hearn my mammy say dat when she come from Virginny dat she come on a boat built outten logs. She say she never was so sick in all her life. I seed a 'hole wagon load of slaves come through our farm one day what was on dere way to Arkansas. Dey was de mos' I ever seed travel at de same time.

"De white folks didn't 'low us to even look at a book. Dey would scol' an' sometimes whup us iffen dey caught us wid our head in a book. Dat is one thang I sho'ly did want to do an' dat was to learn to read an' write. Massa Jim promised to teach us to read an' write, but he neber had de time.

"Dere wan't but one chu'ch on de place what I lived on, an' de colored and de white both went to hit. You know we was neber 'lowed to go to chu'ch widoutten some of de white folks wid us. We wan't even 'lowed to talk wid nobody from anudder farm. Iffen you did, you got one of de wus' whuppin's of your life. Atter freedom Massa Jim tol' us dat dey was 'fraid we'd git together an' try to run away to de No'th, an' dat was w'y dey didn' wan' us gittin' together talkin'.

"A few years 'fo' de war my pappy learnt to read de Bible. (Mary Ella apparently forgot her previous comment on penalties for learning to read). Whenever we would go to chu'ch he would read to us an' we'd sing. 'Bout de mos' two pop'lar songs dey sung was 'Steal Away' an' 'I Wonder Whar Good Ol' Dan'el Was.' 'Steal Away' is sech a pop'lar song what ever'body

knows hit. De yuther one is done mought' nigh played out, so I'll sing hit
for you. It goes lack dis:

I wonder whar was good ol' Dan'el,
I wonder whar was good ol' Dan'el,
I wonder whar was thankin' (thinking) Peter,
I wonder whar was thankin' Peter.

(Chorus)

I'm goin' away, goin' away.
I'm goin' away, goin' away.

I wonder whar was weepin' Mary,
I wonder whar was weepin' Mary,
I'm goin' away, I'm goin' away,
I'm goin' away to live forever,
I'll never turn back no mo'.

"De slaves would git tired of de way dey was treated an' try to run away to
de No'th. I had a cousin to run away one time. Him an' anudder fellow had
got 'way up in Virginny 'fo' Massa Jim foun' out whar dey was. Soon as
Massa Jim foun' de whar'bouts of George he went atter him. When Massa
Jim gits to George an' 'em, George pertended lack he didn' know Massa
Jim. Massa Jim as' him, "George don't you know me?' George he say, 'I
neber seed you 'fo' in my life.' Den dey as' George an' 'em whar did dey
come from. George an' dis yuther fellow look up in de sky an' say, 'I come
from above, whar all is love.' Iffen dey had owned dey knowed Massa Jim
he could have brung 'em back home. My pappy tried to git away de same
time as George an' dem did, but he couldn' see how to take all us chillun
wid him, so he had to stay wid us. De blacks an' de whites would have de
terr'bles' battles sometimes. Dat would be when de blacks would slip off to
de No'th an' was caught an' brung back. De paterollers'd ketch de colored
folks an' lock 'em up twell de owner came atter 'em.

"Iffen a slave was cotched out after nine o'clock he was whupped. Dey
didn' 'low nobody out atter it was dark 'lessen he had a pass from de
Massa. One night, 'fo' George an' dis fellow (I disremembers his name, but
I thinks it was Ezra) runned away, George tried to git over to de bunk
whar he lived an' one of de oberseers seen him an' dey put him in de
'nigger box' for three weeks. Jes' as soon as he got out again, George an'

dis Ezra slipped off. Dey had a sign dat dey would give each yuther eve'y night atter sundown. George would hang de lantern in de window, an' den he would take it outen de window an' hang it raght back in dar ag'in. I couldn't never make no sense outen it. I axed him one day whut he was adoin' dat for. He say dat 'fo' long I'd know 'zackly what is all about. Dis was de sign of how long dey have to wait 'fo' dey try to git away.

"Atter de day's work was over, de slaves didn't have nothin' to do but go to bed. In fac', dey didn't feel lack doin' nothin' else. On Satiday dey sot up an' washed so's dey could have some clean clothes to wear de comin' week. We wukked all day, ever' day 'cep'n some Sat'days, we had a half day off den. Us didn' git many an' on'y when us as' for 'em. On Sundays us jes' laid 'roun' 'mos' all day. Us didn't git no pleasure outten goin' to church, 'caze we warn't 'lowed to say nothin'. Sometimes even on Chris'mas us didn't git no res'. I 'members on one Chris'mas us had to build a lime kiln. When us git a holiday us rested. Iffen dere was a weddin' or a funeral on our plantation us went. Odderways we don't go nowhar.

"De war come when I was a big gal. I 'member dat my uncle an' cousin jined in wid de Yankees to hope fight for de freedom. De Yankees come to our place an' runned Massa Jim away an' tuk de house for a horsepittil. Dey tuk all of Massa Jim's clothes an' gived dem to some of dere frien's. Dey burned up all de cotton, hay, peas an' ever'thing dat was in de barns. Dey made de white folks cook for de colored an' den serve 'em while dey et. De Yankees made 'em do for us lak we done for dem. Dey showed de white folks what it was to work for somebody else. Dey stayed on our place for de longes'. When dey did leave, dere warn't a mouthful to eat in de house. When de war was over, Massa Jim told us dat we had to find som'ers else to live. Co'se some of my folks had already gone when he come home. Us lef' Massa Jim's an' moved to anudder farm. We got pay for de wuk what we did on dis yuther place. Raght atter de war de Ku Klux got atter de colored folks. Dey would come to our houses an' scare us mos' to death. Dey would take some of de niggers out an' whup 'em an' dose dat dey didn't whup dey tied up by dere fingers an' toes. Dese Ku Klux would come to our windows at night an' say: 'Your time ain't long acomin'.' De Ku Klux got so bad dat dey would even git us in de daytime. Dey tuk some of de niggers an' throwed 'em in de river to drown. Dey kep' dis up 'twell some folks from de North come down an' put a stop to it.

"I ma'ied Nelson Granberry. De weddin' was private. I don't have no chilluns, but my husban' got fo'. I haven't heered from any of 'em in a long time now. I guess dey all daid.

"Abe Lincoln was de bes' president dat dis country eber had. Iffen it hadn't been for him we'd still be slaves raght now. I don't think so much of Jeff Davis 'caze he tried to keep us slaves. Booker T. Washington was one of de greates' niggers dat ever lived, he always tried to raise de standard of de race.

"I joined the church 'caze de Bible says dat all people should join de church an' be Christians. Jesus Christ set up de church an' said dat ever'body what wanted to be saved to come unto him. Sin is de cause of de world bein' in de fix dat it's in today. De only way to fight sin is to git together. Iffen we can do away wid sin raght now, de world would be a paradise. In de church we learn de will of God an' what he would have us do.

"Dere was no po' white trash in our 'munity; dey was kep' back in de mountains."

Esther Green

Interview with Esther Green
—Ila B. Prine

US CHILLUN WORE SHOES LIKE GROWNUPS

'Aunt' Esther Green, of 554 Texas Street, Mobile, Alabama, was all too
ready to talk about her slavery days in spite of her assertion that she didn't
remember much about the war.

"I was jus' a chile," she says. "You can figure for yourself. Somebody tole
me I was born in 1855, so I couldn't of been very old. I was born in State
Line, Mississippi, and was owned by Edward Davis. He owned my
mother, Rachel Davis and her mother, Melinda Davis. I never did know
who my pappy was 'cause I never did see him.

"To de bes' of my recollections, my whitefolks was allus good to us
niggers. He neber allowed no overseers and he never whipped none of
dem, 'ceptin' maybe a switching once in a while for us littl'luns when we
didn't behave. I never saw a growed up nigger whipped in all my life. Ole
Massa jus' didn't b'lieve in dat. Massa was shorely a good man. Lots of
times he would get us little niggers up on de porch at de big house and
have us dance for him. We sho used to have a big time out on dem big
white porches.

"I never had no work to do myself, 'cause I always stayed in de big house
wid Miss Mary Davis, ole Massa's wife. I was in de house one day and ole
Massa asked me if I wanted to eat at de table wid dem, so I pulled up a
chair and spite of de fact dere was all kinds of good stuff to eat in front of
me, I called for lye hominy. I sho did love dat stuff better'n anything else I
ever et. Ole Massa and de res' of dem jus' laugh fit to kill. I reckon dey
thought I was crazy sho' nuff', but I et hominy jes' de same.

"As to de number of slaves ole Massa had, I never knew. Us had log
cabins to stay in. De cracks was chinked up wid yellow mud to keep de
cold out and de chim'ney was made of straw and de same kind of mud, but
dem cabins was warmer dan de house is nowadays. We didn't have no
furniture 'ceptin' a home-made bed which was nailed to de wall on one
side and two legs out in de middle of de floor. De mattresses was made of

straw and hay. All de cookin' was done on de big open fireplaces what had big potracks to hang de pots on.

"Massa rationed out de food every week and we usually got a peck of meal. We had plenty of 'taters and peas and other vegetables dat we growed on de place. At Chris'mas time, we was give meat and molasses to make cakes. Us always had plenty of plain food. And too, de men would go huntin' at night and come back wid lots of big fat 'possums and rabbits by de dozen, and mos' of de time, dey would even catch a coon. And old Ben, a nigger who had turkey traps, was always bringin' in lots of dem big fat birds.

"De men and women worked in de field all day, but I never picked a bit of cotton all my life. At night de women would spin and weave cloth, but I never did learn to do dat. Den dey would dye de cloth different colors, mostly red and blue though, and make dem into clothes. Us chilluns had a one-piece dress or slip. Our shoes was all homemade too. Massa had one man who tanned de leather. He would take it an put it into a long trough for a long time and den whatever was done dat was supposed to be done to it, he would take it out and cut it and make shoes. Us chilluns' had shoes same as de grown folks.

"On Sundays, we would got to de white folks' church. Dere was a shed built onto de church and we would sit on benches out under de shed and listen to de preacher. De white folks would have lots of big baptizings, but I never did see no niggers baptized den.

"Ole Massa had a big fambly, three boys and six girls. My own ma had eight chilluns. Us was always healthy and never had to have much medicine. 'Bout de only thing I remembers ever takin' was tea made from de root of de china berry tree. It made good tea for worms, but was to be used only at certain times of de moon. My man also used Jerusalem Oak seed for worms. I never fools wid tryin' to doctor nobody's chilluns now-a-days, things is all so different.

"My Grandma, Melinda, and ole Ben and his wife was three ole people Massa freed long time before de war. When all de niggers was freed, Massa called em up to de house and tole dem dat dey was loose to go wherever suited dem, but mos' of dem stayed on de place two or three weeks, and den one mornin' I woke up and all of dem had left durin' de night. I was de only nigger left on de place and I jus' cried and cried, mostly because I was jus' lonesome for some of my own kind to laugh and talk wid.

"I don't remember exactly what I did after de Surrender, but it was about four years afterwards dat I come to Mobile and I been here every since.

I's a member of de Mobile Delaware Baptist Church, but I can't attend very regular 'count of bein' all crippled up wid de rheumatisms. I reckon dat ailing is natural though, cause I been here a long time and I's got forty grandchilluns and more dan dat many great-grandchilluns."

Charles Hayes

Interview with Charles Hayes
—Mary A. Poole, Mobile

SHO' I BELIEVES IN SPIRITS, SAYS CHARLES

"Mistis," said Charles Hayes from his porch in Maysville, near Mobile, Alabama, "I was a little bitty nigger when de war broke out, an' I belonged to Massa Ben Duncan who lived at Day's Landin' on de Alabamy Ribber.

"Marse Ben's house was de regulation plantation wid slave quarters. Most of de things us used was made raght dere on de plantation, sich as: beds, buckets, tools, soap, brogans, breeches, an' chairs. Our mattresses was either made outen cornshucks or cotton bolls. Us cooked on an open fireplace, an' eve'y Sadday night us would go to de big house for supplies. Marse Ben was good to his slaves an' he 'lowed dem to have a little plot of groun' nex' to de cabins whar dey could raise dere own little crop.

"My mammy was a fiel' han' an' my pappy was a mechanic an' he use to be de handy man aroun' de big house, makin' eve'thing f'um churns an' buckets to wagon wheels. My pappy also useta play de fiddle for de white folks dances in de big house, an' he played it for de colored frolics too. He sho could make dat thing sing.

"Us useta have all sorts of cures for de sick people, f'rinstance, us used de Jerusalem weed cooked wid molasses into a candy for to give to de chilluns to git rid of worms. Den us'd bile de root an' make a kinda tea for de stomach worms. You know de kinds dat little puppies an' little chilluns has dat eats all de food dat goes in to de stomach, an' makes de chile or dog eat plenty but don't git no benefits f'um all dey're eatin'. Horehound, dat growed wild in Clarke County, was used for colds. Mullen tea was used for colds an' swollen j'ints. Den dere was de life everlastin' tea dat was also good for colds and horse mint tea dat was good for de chills an' fevers. Co'se, Mistis, us niggers had a regular fambly doctah dat 'tended to us when we was sho 'nough down raght sick, but dese remedies I's tellin' you 'bout us used when warn't nothin' much ailin' us. It was always to de owner's interest, Mistis, to have de niggers in a good, healthy condition.

"Does I believe in spirits, you says? Sho I does. When Christ walked on de water, de Apostles was skeered he was a spirit, but Jesus told dem dat he warn't no spirit, dat he was as 'live as dey was. He tol' 'em dat spirits couldn't be teched, dat dey jus' melted when you tried to. So, Mistis, Jesus musta meant dat dere was sich a thing as spirits.

"Atter de war my pappy an' mammy stayed on de Duncan plantation en' worked on share crops. Dere was a school on de groun's for us slave chilluns, an' my gran'mammy, Salina Duncan, taught de bible, 'ca'se she was f'um Virginny an' had been learnt to read an' write by her Mistis up dere.

"My fus' wife was named Alice Bush, an' us had ten chilluns; my second one was named Caroline Turner an' us didn't have but eight. Both my ole womens is daid now, white folks, an' I stays here wid one of my daughters. You see, my eyesight is almos' gone due to one day when I was a workin' in de forge, a hot piece of iron flew up an' landed in my eye. 'Twarn't long befo' it started to hurtin' in my udder eye. Now both is 'bout to give out."

Adeline Hodges

Personal interview with 'Aunt' Adeline Hodges
3 Frye Street, Mobile, Alabama
—Ila B. Prine, [HW: Mobile?]

HONGRY FOR PUN'KIN PIE

'Aunt' Adeline, a tall, gaunt, bright-skinned Negro woman, lives on Frye St., Mobile, Ala. The day I called she was nodding in a cane bottom rocking chair on a wide porch that extended across the front of a cottage almost hidden in a grove of giant oaks. She opened her eyes, which were covered by a pair of steel-rimmed glasses with one lens badly cracked. The news that a search was being made for old people who had lived during slavery days acted like an electric shock on the old woman, who immediately sat up straight and said:

"Lor, yes'm, I libed in dose days, and I tells you I 'members all 'bout dem. Do come in and set down. De fust white people I b'longed to was a man named Jones, who was a colonel in de war, but I can't tell you much 'bout dem, 'caze I was jes' a li'l gal den. I was jes' big 'nuff to tote water to de fiel' to de folks wukking and to min' de gaps in de fence to keep de cattle out when dey was gatherin' de crops. I don't 'spec' you knows anything 'bout dose kind of fences. Dey was built of rails and when dey was gatherin' de crops dey jes' tuk down one section of de fence, so de wagons could git through.

"A'ter de war broke out ole Mister Jones went off to hit, and I 'members de day he lef'. He come to de fiel' to tell all de han's goodbye, wid a big white plume on his hat. Dat was in Bolivar County, Mississippi. A'ter ol' Mister Jones lef' for de war, den de nigger drivers an' oberseer begun to drive us 'round lack droves of cattle. Every time dey would hyar de Yankees was coming dey would take us out in de woods and hide us. Finally dey sold us a'ter carrying us away from Bolivar County. Some of us was sold to people in Demopolis, Alabama, an' Atlanta, Georgia, an' some to folks in Meridian and Shubuta, Mississippi. I don't any more know whar my own folks went to dan you does.

"I 'members afore leaving ole Mister Jones' place how dey grabbed up all de chillun dat was too li'l to walk and puttin' us in wagons. Den de older folks had to walk, and dey marched all day long. Den at night dey would strike camp. I has seen de young niggers what was liable to run away wid dere legs chained to a tree or de wagon wheels. Dey would rake up straw and throw a quilt ober hit and lie dat way all night, while us chillun slep' in de wagons.

"When us come to de big river at Demopolis, Alabama, I 'members seein' de big steamboats dere, and dey said dat de sojers was goin' away on dem. Hit was in Demopolis us was sold, and a man name Ned Collins of Shubuta, Mississippi, bought me."

'Aunt' Adeline said that the houses the slaves lived in on the Jones plantation were board houses, and that Mr. Jones owned a big plantation and lots of slaves. She said that they had home-made beds, nailed to the walls, with mattresses made out of shucks.

After having been sold to Mr. Collins, of Shubuta, Mississippi, 'Aunt' Adeline said that life was very hard, not so much for herself, but she saw how hard the other slaves worked. She was the house girl and helped clean house, wash dishes, and take care of the children. After finishing that work, she had to spin thread. Each day she would have to spin so many cuts, and if she did not finish the required number, she was punished.

She said that her mistress kept the finished work on top of a large wardrobe, and 'Aunt' Adeline said that many times she would steal a cut of thread off that wardrobe to complete the day's task to keep from being punished.

As she grew older she did have to go to the field and pick cotton. 'Aunt' Adeline does not remember it pleasantly. She said:

"I jes' hates to hab to weigh anything today, 'caze I 'members so well dat each day dat de slaves was given a certain number of pounds of cotton to pick. When weighing up time come and you didn't hab de number of pounds set aside, you may be sho' dat you was goin' to be whupped. But hit wasn't all bad times 'caze us did hab plenty to eat, 'specially at hog killin' time. Dey would hab days ob hog killin' and de slaves would bake dere bread and come wid pots, pepper, and salt. A'ter cleanin' de hogs, dey would gib us de livers and lights, and us would cook dem ober a fire out in de open and hit sho' was good eatin'. De usual 'lowance a week of pickled pork was six or seven pounds, and iffen you had a big family of chillun dey gib you more. Den dey gib you a peck of meal, sweet 'taters, sorghum syrup, and plenty of buttermilk. At Christmas times, dey gib you extra syrup to make cakes wid and sweet 'taters to make 'tater pone. And, Lor', dey would hab big cribs of pun'kins. Hit makes me hongry to think 'bout dem good ol' pun'kin pies.

"And did dey raise chickens? You knows in Mississippi dat de minks was bad 'bout killin' dem. I 'members one time de minks got in de chicken house and killed nearly every chicken on de place. Ole Mister Jones had de cook to clean and cook dem, and he come out in de fiel' an' eat wid dem to let de slaves know dat hit was all right. Den us had dem good ol' cushaws and lye hominy, too.

"De clothes was made out ob homespun in one piece. I 'members I allus had mine split up de side so I could git 'bout in a hurry. De women had pantalettes made and tied to dere knees to wear in de fields to keep de dew off dere legs. De shoes was made of cow hide and was called red russets. De way dey got dem darker was to take a hog 'gristle' and hang up in de chimbley. When hit git full of soot, we rub de shoes wid dat. Den dey used de darker shoes for dere Sunday best.

"You asked me about huntin'? Lor', yes dey hunted in dem times. Up in dem swamps in Mississippi dere was bears as big as cows, and deers aplenty. Dey bofe was bad about comin' in de corn fiel's and tearin' down de corn. You could hyar dem at nights out in de fiel's. Dey also caught plenty of possums and coons.

"Of course, us got sick, but dey had de doctor. In dose days de doctor would cup you and bleed you. I seen a many a person cupped. De doctor had a li'l square lookin' block of wood wid tiny li'l knifes attached to hit. On top was a trigger lack is on a gun, and de doctor would put de block of wood at de nape of dere neck an' pull dat trigger. Den he hab a piece of cotton wid somepin' on hit to stop de blood when he had cupped you long 'nough. Dey would allus gib us calamus (calomel) to clean us out, and den de nex' mawnin' dey gib us a big bowl of gruel made out ob meal and milk. Den us'd be all right.

"De slaves warn't 'lowed to go to church, but dey would whisper 'roun' and all meet in de woods and pray. De only time I 'members my pa was one time when I was a li'l chile, he set me on a log by him an' prayed, an' I knows dat was whar de seeds ob religion was planted in my min'. Today

I's happy to tell folks 'bout Jesus and thank Him for His goodness to me.
Hit won't be long twell I meet Him face to face and thank Him."

Caroline Holland

Interview with Caroline Holland
—Mabel Farrior

CAROLINE HOLLAND HAD MANY MASTERS

"Yassuh, I was a slave," spoke Aunt Carry from her vine-shaded porch at
No. 3 Sharpe Street, Montgomery, Alabama. "I was borned in 1849 on Mr.
Will Wright's plantation on the Mt. Meigs road. Massa Will had a big
slave house an' us niggers sho' use to have a good time playin' 'roun' down
at de slave quarters. We had a row of houses two stories high, an' dey was
filled wid all sorts of niggers. When I was twelve year old, I was made
nu'ss fer my mistis's little girl an' at de fus' I couldn't do nothin' but rock de
cradle. I didn't know how to hol' de baby. Us niggers had gardeens
(guardians) dat look 'atter us lak dey did atter de hosses and cows and
pigs.

"One night atter we had all gone to bed I heered a noise at de window, an'
when I look up dere was a man a climbin' in. He was a nigger. I could tell
eben do I could scarce see him, I knowed he was a nigger. I could hear my
mistis a breathin', an' de baby was soun' asleep too. I started to yell out but
I thought dat de nigger would kill us so I jes' kep' quiet. He come in de
window, an' he see us a sleepin' dere, an' all of a sudden I knowed who it
was. 'Jade,' I whispers, 'What you a doin' here?' He come to my bed and
put his rough han' ober my mouf.

"Listen you black pickaninny, you tell em dat you saw me here an' I'll kill
you,' he say, 'I th'ow yo' hide to de snakes in de swamp. Now shet up.'

"Wid dat he went to de dresser an' taken mistis' money bag. Atter dat he
went to de window an' climb down de ladder an' I didn't do nothin' but
shake myself nearly to death fum fright. De nex' day de oberseer an' de
pattyrollers went a searchin' th'ough de slave quarters an' dey foun' de
money bag under Jade's cot. Dey tuk him an' whupped him for near fifteen
minutes. We could hear him holla way up at de big house. Jade, he neber
got ober dat whuppin'. He died three days later. He was a good nigger,
'peer to me lak, an' de bes' blacksmith in de whole county. I ke'pa-
wonderin' whut made him want ter steal dat purse. Den I foun' out later dat
he was a goin' to pay a white man ter carry him ober de line to de No'thern
States. Jade jus' had too big ideas fo' a nigger. I us'ta see Jade's ghos' a

walkin' out in de garden in de moonlight; sometime he sit on de fence an'
look at his ole cabin, den sometimes he stroll off down de cotton fiel'.
When de Lawd git th'ough a punishin' him fo' a stealin' dat money, I guess
he won't make us no mo' visits. He jus' go right on in heaben. Dat's what
ghos'tes is, you know; peoples dat can't quite git in heaben, an' dey hadda
stroll 'roun' little longer on de outside repentin'.

"Soon atter dat my gardeen tuk me to Tallasse when de massa died. My
gardeen was a good man. He was always a-makin' speeches fo' de slaves
to stay under bondage till dey was twenty-one. One dey he was in front of
a sto' talkin' 'bout de slaves an' a man come up to him an' said he don't like
de way Capt. Clanton talk (dat was my gardeen's name). Capt. Clanton ask
him whut he goin' ter do 'bout it an' de man tuk out a pistol an' kil't de
Cap'n raght dere on de spot.

"Den I was sold to another man, a Mr. Williamson, 'bout de time de war
broke loose, an' Massa Williamson tuk me ober ter lib wid some mo'
peoples. He said he had mo' slaves dan he could take keer of. Dis was de
Abernathy plantation. While de massa was a standin' in de slave quarters a
takin' to Mr Abernathy, I noticed a boy wid a bad eye. I didn't lak him at
all an' I tol' de massa I don't wanna stay, kaze I didn't lak de way dat boy
Lum wid de bad eye looked at me. Den Mr. Abernathy brung a boy 'bout
sebenteen year old; a big strong lookin' boy named Jeff. He say 'Jeff, look
out after Carry here. Don't let her git into no trouble.' Fum dat time on till
'bout five year ago, Jeff he always look after me, kaze atter de war I ma'ied
him. Now I ain't got nobody but myself."

Joseph Holmes

I
Personal interview with Joseph Holmes
Grand Avenue, Prichard, Alabama
—Ila B. Prine, Mobile, Alabama

DEY KEP' NIGGERS IN GOOD CONDITION TO SELL

Standing in the middle of the road at Prichard, suburb of Mobile, and gesticulating while talking to a small group of interested listeners an old Negro man ended his talk to the small gathering and punctuated his last sentence with a spat of tobacco.

"No'm," he continued after I had put in my appearance and asked him a question, "I doesn't know whether I was a slave, but jus' de same I seed Gen'l Grant's army when it went th'ough Virginny. Jus' as sho' as you is standin' dar, lady, I seed dem mens all dressed in blue suits, a-marching' side by side, gwine down de road pas' our place. It tuk 'em three days to go by our house.

"An' I remembers when dem Yankees came to our ole Mistis' house an' take a ladder an' clumb up to de roof an' tear de boards outter de ceilin' to git dem big hams an' shoulders my white folks done had hid up dar. When de Yankees find dat stuff dey give it all to de niggers. Den atter de solgers lef' ole Miss called us to her an' tol' us we was free, but for us to give back some of de meat an' things dat de Yankees done give us, 'ca'se she didn't have nothin' to eat 'roun' de place. 'Course we was glad to do it, 'ca'se Mistis sho' was good to us.

"I remembers ebery Sunday mawnin' dat she'd make de older slaves bring all de little niggers up to de big house, so she could read de Bible to 'em, and den she give us plenty of dem good biscuits and taters dat Susanne cook for us. She'd say: 'Git 'roun' dere, Susanne, and he'p dem little niggers' plates.' I really thought Mistis was a angel.

"Talkin' 'bout niggers bein' free. Ole Miss tol' us was free, but it was ten or twelve years atter de surrender befo' I knowed whut she meant. I was a big boy goin' to school befo' I had an understandin' as to what she meant.

"Ole Miss taught de niggers how to read an' write an' some of 'em got to be too good at it, 'ca'se dey learned how to write too many passes so's de pattyrollers wouldn't cotch 'em, an' on dem occasions was de onlyes' times dat I ever seed one of our niggers punished.

"Mistis never 'lowed no mistreatin' of de slaves, 'case dey was raisin' slaves for de market, an' it wouldn't be good bizness to mistreat 'em. Lor' Miss, my white folks was rich; dey had as many as five or six hundred niggers; men, women an' chilluns. De plantation was big, but I doesn't remember how many acres it was, but I does remember dat de cabins was all built in rows, an' dere was streets laid out among de cabins. De chimneys was built outten dirt an' sticks, an' you know up in Virginny it got powerful cold, so when dey built de cabins dey th'owed dirt up under 'em to keep de wind an' snow out.

"I was bawn in Henry County, Virginny, near Danville, an' I's been to Vicksburg an' Petersburg a many a time wid my pappy to de wheat an' 'bacca market. Lor', honey, Virginny is de bes' place on earth for good eaten' an' good white folks. If anybody tells you dat de white folks was mean to dere niggers, dey neber come from Virginny, 'case us was too near de free states, an' I done already tol' you dat dey raised niggers to sell an' dey kep' 'em in good condition. In dose days white folks an' black folks was black folks. Jus' lak Booker T. Washington was a riber between de niggers of dis generation an' learnin'. He had all dat was fine an' good, an' he give de bes' to his people iffen dey would take it. Dat was de way wid de white folks den; dey didn't do no whuppin'.

"I's de onlyes' rat lef' in de pond, an' 'case I ain't hung in de smoke house, folks thinks I's not as old as I say I is, but chile, I's been here a long time. I 'members how black Sam useta preach to us, an' when I growed up I useta think warnt nobody Christians cep'n us Babtists, but I know better now, an' de longer I lives de mo' I realizes dat de churches go 'way 'case dey leaves off de ordinances of God, although us has a Bible an' mo' Christian readin' dan ever befo'.

"My mammy's name was Eliza Rowlets an' my pappy's was Joseph Holmes. My pappy had de same name as de peoples dat owned him an' my gran'mammy name was Lucy Holmes. Gran'mammy Holmes lived to be over a hundred years old, an' she was de fust pusson I ever seed daid. In dem days it tuk three days to bury a pusson, 'case dey dug de graves as deep as de corpse was tall.

"Land sakes a-livin', us had great times, an' I forgot to tell you dat us had home-made beds wid two sides nailed to de wall an' de mattresses was made outen wheat straw.

"As for huntin' I done plenty of it an' one thing I got to git forgiveness for was when I lef' Virginny, I lef' 'bout fifty or sixty snares set to cotch rabbits an' birds.

"My mammy had eight chilluns an' we was raised in pairs. I had a sister who come along wid me, an' iffen I jumped in de river she done it too. An' iffen I go th'ough a briar patch, here she come along too.

"'Bout de fruit; it makes my mouth water to think about dem cheese apples, dat was yaller lak gold, an' dose Abraham apples, an' de cherry tree as big as dese oaks here. I's eaten many a big sugar and sweetheart cherry. But dere was another kind called de Gorilla dat growed as big as de yaller plums down dis way. Now let me tell you somp'n 'bout Virginny; 'dey had dere laws 'bout drink. Dey had de bes' peach an' cherry brandy an' mos' any kin' you eber heared of, but dey didn't 'low you to make drink outten anything you could make bread wid; sich as corn or rye. Us had our brandy same as you would coffee, 'case it was cold, an' some mawnin's my pappy would git de brandy out an' my mammy would putt a little water an' sugar wid it an' gib it to us chilluns. Us neber thought nothin' 'bout drinkin'. I kinda believes lak dat ole infidel Ingersoll who said dat anything dat was a custom was dere religion.

"Now you axed about hog-killin' time? Dat was de time of times. For weeks de mens would haul wood an' big rocks, an' pile 'em together as high as dis house, an' den have several piles lak dat 'roun' a big hole in de groun' what had been filled wid water. Den jus' a little atter midnight, de boss would blow de ole hawn, an' all de mens would git up an' git in dem pig pens. Den dey would sot dat pile of wood on fire an' den start knockin' dem hogs in de haid. Us neber shot a hog lak us does now; us always used an axe to kill 'em wid. Atter knockin' de hog in de haid, dey would tie a rope on his leg an' atter de water got to de right heat, fum dose red-hot rocks de hog would be throwed in an' drug aroun' a while, den taken out an' cleaned. Atter he was cleaned he was cut up into sections an' hung up in de smoke house. Lawsie, lady, dey don't cure meat dese days; dey jus' uses some kind of liquid to brush over it. We useta have sho' 'nuff meat.

"Den come cawnshuckin' time. My goodness, I would jus' love to be dar now. De cawn would be piled up high an' one man would git on dat pile. It was usually a kinda nigger foreman who could sing an' git de work outten de niggers. Dis fo'man would sing a verse somp'n lak dis:

Polk and Clay went to war,
Polk come back wid a broken jaw.

Den all de niggers would sing back at him wid a kinda shoutin' sound. Near 'bout all de times de fo'man made up his own songs, by pickin' dem outen dat shuckin'! It war de jug dat dey brung aroun' eve'y hour. Dat's de onlyes' time de slaves really got drunk.

"In dem ole days I went to plenty of dances an' candy pullin's durin' de Yule season, but I doesn't do dat no mo'. I's a preacher an' when I fus' lef' Virginny, I come to Georgy an' stayed dar twenty years whar I kicked up plenty of dus'. I even taught school dar. Den I come to Alabamy an' lived in Evergreen for 'bout twenty mo' years. Since I been in Mobile I's worked for sich men as ole Simon, Damrich, an' Van Antwerp, an' all dere chilluns has been in dese here arms of mine. I's been a square citizen an' dere hasn't been a time dat I is had to call on nobody but Uncle Sam when ole man 'pression cotched me. But thank de Lawd I is still able to git about an' have all my senses 'cep' my eye-sight, an' it's jus' a little po'ly. I is got all my teeths 'cep' one, an' my mammy was always proud of my hair. See how silky an' fine it is? Not quite white, dough. I hope I lives long enough for it to turn white as snow. I think St. Peter will lak it better dat way."

II
Personal interview with Joseph Holmes
Grand Avenue, Prichard, Alabama
—*Ila B. Prine, Mobile, Alabama*

TWELVE YEARS 'TWELL I UNDERSTOOD SURRENDER

In the middle of the road near Prichard, an incorporated suburb of Mobile, stood an aged Negro man, gesticulating as he told a tale of other days to a small audience. Tall, straight, with gray hair and mustache, he was a picturesque figure. He does not know whether he was born in slavery, he said, but he knows his age to be about eighty-one.

"I doesn't know whether I was a slave, but jes' de same I seed Gineral Grant's army when hit went th'ough Virginny," he said "Jes' as sho' as yo' is standin' dar, lady, I seed him, and I seed dem men all dressed in dem blue suits a-marchin' side by side, gwine down de road pas' our place. Hit tuk dem three days tuh git pas' our house.

"An' does I 'member when dem Yankees come tuh Ol' Mistiss house an' tuk a ladder an' clim' up tuh de roof an' tear de boards outta de ceilin' tuh git dem big hams an' shoulders dey had hid up dar? I sho' does. De women folks makes de slaves hide wid de meat; an' when dem Yankees fin' dat stuff dey jes' gib hit all tuh de niggers, an' I 'members too, how Ol' Miss calls us all to her atter dey lef' an' tole us dat us was free, but she tole us dat us hab tuh gib back ob de meat an' 'serves 'case she didn't hab a bit tuh eat. 'Cose we was glad tuh do hit 'case Ol' Miss sho' was good tuh her slaves.

"I 'members ebery Sunday mawnin' dat she made de older slaves bring all de little niggers up to her big white, two-story house, so she could read de Bible to us, an' den she gib us plenty dem good biscuits an' 'taters dat she had de cook, Susanne, cook for us. She'd say 'Git 'roun' dere, Susanne, an' he'p dem li'l niggers plates,' I, railly thought Ol' Miss was an angel.

"Talkin 'bout niggers bein' freed, Ol' Miss tole us us was free, but hit was ten or twelve years atter de Surrender, befo' I knowed whut she was talkin' 'bout. I was a big boy goin' to school befo' I had any understanin' as tuh whut she meant.

"Ol' Miss taught de niggers how to read an' write, an' some ob dem got to
be too 'ficient wid de writin', 'case dey larn how tuh write too many passes
so de pattyrollers wudn't git dem. Dat was de onliest time I ebber knowed
Ol' Miss tuh hab de slaves punished.

"Ol' Miss nebber 'lowed no mistreatin' de slaves, case dey was raisin'
slaves for de market, an' hit wouldn't be good business to mistreat 'em.
Lor' mah white folks was rich; dey had as many as five or six hundred
niggers, men, women and chillun. De plantation was big but I don't
'member how many acres I does 'member de cabins was all built in rows,
an' streets was laid out 'tween de cabins. De chimbeys was built outta dirt
an' sticks, an' sticks, an' yo' know up in Virginny hit got turrible cold an'
de snow would pile up, so when de cabins was built, de men th'owed dirt
up under de house to keep de snow an' cold out. Yo' might think dat dirt
would wash out from under de house, but hit didn't. Hit jes' made dem so
warm an' com'fo'ble we did'nt suffer.

"Dat was de way wid de white folks den; dey didn't do no whippin' an'
mistreatin' ob de slaves. Oh, once in a while Ol' Miss might slap de cook's
face an' tell her tuh bear down 'roun' dere, an' if she wanted de servin' boys
to hurry, she would say 'Cutch hit,' meanin' fer dem to cut some steps an'
git 'bout in a hurry.

"I's de ol'est rat in de pon', an' 'case I ain't hung in de smokehouse, folks
think I's not as ol' as I says I is, but chile, I's been heah. I 'members how
Sam useta to preach to us, when we was at Ol' Miss's place, an' when I
growed up, I 'members how I useta think nobody was a Christian 'ceptin'
us Baptists, but I knows better now. An' de longer I lib de mo' I realize dat
de chu'ches go away 'case dey leabes off de ordinances ob God, 'tho us has
got de Bible an' mo' Christian litterchoor dan eber befo'.

"My ma's name was 'Liza Rowlets, an' mah daddy's name was Joseph
Holmes. My daddy had de same name as de people whut owned him, an'
my gran'ma's name was Lucy Holmes. Gran'ma Lucy libed to be a
hundred yeahs old, an' she was de fust pusson I ebber seed daid. Hit tuk
three days tuh bu'y a pusson den, 'case dey dug de graves as deep as yo' is
tall, which means mo' than five feet deep. Lor' sakes a-livin' us had great
times. I forgot tuh tell yo' dat us had home-made beds wid two sides nailed
tuh de wall, an' de mattresses was made outta wheat straw. Dat's 'minds
me dat dere wa'n't no pore cattle in dem times, 'case yo' could go whar dey
thresh de wheat an' git all de straw yo' wanted an' feed de dry cattle on hit.

An' you wouldn't believe de fruit us did hab! Yo don't nebber see de like down dis way. Sich as apples, cherries, quinces, peaches an' pears.

"As fer huntin', I done plenty of it, an' one thing I got to git forgiveness fer was when I lef' Virginny, I lef' 'bout sixty or seventy snares set to ketch rabbits an' birds.

"My ma had eight chillun an' we was raised in pairs. I had a sister who come along wid me, an' if I jumped in de ribber tuh swim, she did hit too; if I clum' a tree, or went th'ough a briar patch, she done hit right behin' me. Ma wanted to know why her clo's was so tore up, an' when dey was pretty, we'd make hit right wid Ma by havin' a rabbit or coon wid us, an' sometimes a mud turtle. An' as fer 'possums an' coons, us ketch dem in plenty.

"'Bout de fruit, hit makes mah mouf watah tuh think 'bout dem cheese apples dat was yaller lac' gold, an' dose Abraham apples de lack of which ain't now to be had. An' dose cherry trees as big as dese oaks, wid long limbs an' big sugar an' sweetheart, an' black heart cherries. Den dere was annudder kin' of cherry called de gorilla, dat was roun' an' growed as big as de yaller plums down dis way.

"Now, let me tell yo' sumpin' 'bout Virginny. Hit had hits own law 'bout drink. Dey made de bes' peach an' cherry brandy an' mos' any kin' yo' ebber heerd ob, 'ceptin' dey didn't 'low yo' to make drink out ob anythin' you could make into bread. Now yo' understan's, sich as corn and rye.

"Us had our brandy same as yo' would coffee, 'case hit was cold an' some mawnin's us would git up an' de snow would be halfway up de do', an' de men would hab to ditch hit out, so us could git out of de house. On dem rail cold mawnin's my daddy would git de brandy out an' my ma wud put a li'l water an' sugar wid hit an gib to us chillun. An' den she'd take some in her mouf' an' put hit in de baby's mouf an' hit wud open hits eyes an' stamp hits foot rail peart lack.

"Us nebber thought nothin' of drinkin'. I kinda believes lack dat ol' infidel, Ingersoll, who said dat anythin' dat was de custom, was de religion.

"Folks was a heap kinder-hearted den dey is now, 'case dey kep' big dogs to hunt up people los' in de snow. Dey all seemed mo' happy 'case dey was all busy. At night instid of wastin' dey time, dey wud go tuh de big house an' spin an' weave an' make clo's.

"I kin hyar dat ol' loom hummin' now, an' see great cards ob cloth comin' out, an' dem was clo's den dat was made from hit. Hit tuck fire tuh git dem offen' yo' dey was so strong. I doesn't 'member whut dey used fer dye, but I knows dey used copperas as sizin' to hol' de colors. Some of de cloth was dyed red, blue an' black. I jes' can't 'member 'bout de dye, but dey used copperas. 'Dat was the qualification of de intelligence ob de primitive age', in usin' dat copperas. Dey not only made our clo's, but also made out hats. Of co'se dey wa'n't very hatty, but was mo' cappy. Dey made 'em wid tabs ober de ears, an' to tie under de chin, an' was dey warm, I'll say!

"Now, when yo' axes 'bout hawg killin' time, dat was de time! Fer weeks de men would haul wood and big rocks, an' pile hit all together as high as dat house; den hab sev'ral piles like dese 'roun' a big hole in de groun' whut had been filled wid watah. Den jes' a li'l atter mid-night de boss would blow de ol' horn, an' all de men would git up an' git in dem hog pens. Den dey would set dat pile of wood on fire, an' den start knockin' dem hawgs in de haid. Us nebber shot a hawg like dey does now. Us allus used an ax to kill 'em wid.

"Atter knockin' de hawg in de haid, dey would tie a rope on hits leg, an atter de water got to de right heat from dose red hot rocks whut had been pushed out ob dat pile ob nu'in wood into de watah, dey wud th'ow de hog in an' drag hit aroun' awhile, an' take him out an' hab him clean in 'bout three pair o' minutes. Atter he was clean dey hung him up, an' den later cut him up an' hung him in de smoke house, an' smoke him wid great oak logs. Huh, dey don't cu'ah meat now, dey jes' use sum kinda brush an' liquid, but dey don't hab meat lack us did.

"Den come co'shuckin' time. Mah goodness, I jes' would love to be dere now. De co'n would be piled up high an' one man would git on dat pile. Hit usually was one who was kinda niggah fo'man dat could sing an' get de wuck out of de odder niggers. Dis fo'man would sing a verse somethin' lack dis:

Polk an' Clay went to War,
An' Polk come back wid a broken jar.

"Den all de niggers would sing back to him, an' hallo, a kinder shoutin' soun'. Ginerally dis fo'man made up his songs by pickin' dem up from whut he had heard white folks tell of wars. But Miss yo' know whut was de motor powah of dat co'n shuckin'? Hit was de ol' jug dat was brung 'roun' ebery hour. Dat's de onliest time any ob de slaves railly got drunk.

"I wish I could 'member dose ol' songs, but all dat hallo done lef' me, 'case de onliest singin' I hears now is de good ol' sisters singin' an' sayin' 'Amen.'

"In days gone by I went to plenty of dances an' candy pullin's but I doesn't do dat any mo'. I's a preacher, an' when I fu'st lef' Virginny I come to Georgia an' stayed dere twenty yeahs, an' I kicked up a plenty of dust in Georgia. I eben taught school an' built a plenty of chu'ches dere. Den I come on to Alabammy, an' libed in Evergreen fo' about twenty mo' yeahs, an' I built a two-story brick chu'ch dere. Since I's been in Mobile I's wu'ked by dat Bienville Squah for twenty-eight years, for sich men as ol' man Simon, Damrich, an' Van Antwerp, an' all dere chillun has been in dese arms. I's been a squah citizen an' dere hasn't been but one time in mah life I's had to call on anybody, an' dat was when I had tuh call on Uncle Sam when ol' man Depression got me. But thank God I's still able to be 'bout an' have all my faculties, 'ceptin' my eyesight is a li'l porely. I still has all mah teeth, 'ceptin' one, an' my ma allus tuck pride in mah haih, yo' see how fine an' silky hit is, an' hit ain't snow white yit. Dere is one thing to be thankful fer. Dat is 'case I's so near home."

Josh Horn

Interview with Josh Horn
—Ruby Pickens Tartt, Livingston, Alabama

CHASING GUINEA JIM, THE RUNAWAY SLAVE

Seven miles East from Livingston on State Road No. 80, thence Left two
miles via a dim road through the woods to a cultivated section, the
beginning of a large plantation area, stands the old-timey cabin of Josh
Horn, a well known and influential figure in the colored community.
Vigorous and active despite his more than 80 years, Josh exemplifies the
gentleness with which time deals with those dwelling in a healthful spot
and living the simple lives of a rural people. I found him nodding on his
front steps.

"Josh," I said, "I've come to get you to tell me some old war-time stories,
and I want to ask you some questions about you and Alice and how you-
all are getting along. I just want to know all about you and your family as
far back as you can remember."

"All right, Miss Ruby, I's glad to tell you what I knows," said Josh, "and it
ain't gonna be a lot of fibbin', but jes' lak everything was. I's telling you
lak you axed me.

"Now, 'bout how us is getting along. I's telling you de troof, ef I was took
'fore God, I'd say jes' lak I's saying now, ef my chillun ever et a moufful
dat wasn't honest, dey et it somewhar else, 'ca'se I ain't ever stole a
moufful somepin' t'eat for 'em in all my life. It's honest vittles dey et, and
varmints I's killed in de woods, 'ca'se us raised chillun fast, and us had a
heap of 'em, sixteen, if I 'members right, and soon's I found out dat I could
help feed 'em dat way, I done a heap of hunting. And everybody knows I's
a good hunter. Alice used to make me go every Friday night; den us
always had a 'possum or two for Sunday."

"Why," I asked, "didn't you go Saturday night?"

"Well, I'll tell you," Josh said, "Alice is a good Christian woman, and she
knowed I'd hunt mighty nigh all night, and she didn't want nobody see me
coming in Sunday morning wid no gun and no dogs; so I went every

Friday night and went in de week too, and dat holp a lot to feed de chillun. I don't owe nobody, not a nickel.

"I lak to got in debt, when de Government come in and tried to help us wid dat cotton doings. Dey cut it down so on me, tell I couldn't make nothing; but I's getting on all right now, and so is my chillun. Us is got fourteen living, and dey's all been to school, but ain't but one been to Booker Washington's school, but dey kin all read and write, and some of 'em teaching school out here in de country. De doctor, he come clear out here to see us, 'ca'se I always pays him. He jes' here wid Alice last night. It's nine mile and two of dem's back here in de woods through Marse Johnnie's place, but he come when us went atter him 'bout midnight, and dat's a comfort to know he come."

I asked, what was the matter with Alice.

"Well, I'll tell you, Miss Ruby. She was back dere wid me in de kitchen, and I got through eating and I come out and set down in de swinger to git some air. De moon was shining, and Alice come out, saying loud as she could: 'Who is you? Who is you?' De chillun run to her wid a lamp and I run, and 'twan't nobody dere. Well, Alice said 'twas a big man standing right 'side her dressed in black, and she called it Death. Us couldn't do nothing wid her, and she didn't know nobody, me nor de chillun, so I went to Livingston atter Dr. McCain, and he come and set wid her 'bout a hour. He said 'twas de 'cute 'digestion or somepin' lak dat. I knowed 'twan't no sperrit; I don't b'lieve in nothing lak dat."

"Well," I said, "I don't know, Josh, I've been hearing some ghost tales that freeze the blood in my veins."

"Yassum," said Josh, "if you wants to hear ghost tales, I kin sho tell 'em, ca'se I seed dis here wid my own eyes. 'Tain't no made-up nothing, needer; jes' somepin' I seed jes' lak I tells you.

"Green Hale and Isham Mathews b'longed to New Hope church, and de Reverend Bird Hall pastored dere. Dey axed me down to hear him preach one night, and us three, me and Green and Isham, was riding along side and side. I's riding a mule, but it was a fast mule, and Green couldn't keep up, en Isham said: 'Somebody been hunting.' I looked up and 'twas a sapling right 'cross de road. He said, 'Fellow oughten leave nothing lak dat. When de moon git low, it hit him in de face.' De moon was straight up and down den, and I said: 'Dat's right', and I's telling you de troof, dat sapling jes' riz up, turned aroun' in de air, en de brush part tickled my mule and Isham's hoss in de face. If you ever seed 'em buck and rare and jump up, dey sho did. Den dey took off down de road, and we didn't hold 'em back, and here come Green. We lef' him behind, 'cause his mule couldn't keep up. If you ever heard a man pray more earnester dan old Green, I ain't! He come down de road a-yelling: 'Lord, us live togedder, let us die togedder.' He meant for us to wait on him, but I couldn't hold dat mule, and I wan't trying to hold him! I was gitting away from dar!

"When us come togedder, us was a mile from whar us done been, den us had to decide what to do. Isham said for us to go wid him, and Green said no, us nearer to his house; but us wan't near to nobody and I was so scared, hadn't been for Alice, I'd a jes' stayed right whar us was 'tell sun-up. I said, 'No, every man better take keer his own self,' en us did. When I got home, I didn't take nothing off dat mule but myself. I jes' left him standing at de do' wid de saddle on. What skeered Green so, was a man, he said, what was ridin' right 'side him en didn't have no head! 'Twas a good thing he didn't tell me dat den, I'd jes' nacherly drap dead!

"No'm, I don't 'zackly believes in ghosties, but I heared Mr. Marshall Lee say he was riding on home one night and a woman stepped out in de road and say: 'Marshall, let me ride.' He say: 'My hoss won't tote double.' She say: 'Yes it will,' and she jump up behind him, and dat hoss bucked and jumped nigh 'bout from under him, but when he got home, she wan't dere. He say, his sister had jes' died and it mout been her.

"'Nother time, one Friday night, Alice say us better git a 'possum for Sunday. She say she didn't want none caught atter midnight on Sadday. I went down whar I knowed dey was 'simmons, and dem dogs never treed nothing; dey jes' run 'round dat 'simmon tree lak dey gone crazy. I'm telling you de troof, somepin' jump outer dat tree, had a head back'erds and for'erds and look lak a flame shooting out it eyes! 'Twan't lak no possum I ever seed, 'twan't lak nothing. Dem dogs, Liz and Roger en Cuba, made a bluge at me. Cotton was waist high, and I run down de cotton row and cross de road and dey trail me. I say: 'What ail you, dogs?' And dey jes' come on a-barkin', and dey run me to de bridge over Konkabyer. So I clumb on de banisters. I seed dey had my trail an dey gonna ketch me, so I turn 'round and tore out for de slough. Dey lost my trail dere and when I got home, 'bout daylight, de thorns and de briars and all done tore my clothes plum off me. 'Twas t'ree days 'fore I ever seed dem dogs ag'in.

"And I kin tell you somepin' else. It's jes' lak I say, I's always been a hunter, en one night I went down in de post oak woods hunting by myself. Dis is a fact; 'tain't no lie. It's what I done. I had a mighty good dog, and I jes' kept walking and walking, and I got mighty nigh to Mr. Redhead Jim Lee's place, and I walked on and atter while I seed I'd lost my dog. I couldn't see him nowhar and I couldn't hear him nowhar, and den somepin' say to me, jes' lak dis: 'Josh, blow your horn!' Jes' lak dat, lak somebody talking to me. Well I give three loud, long blows and set dere awhile longer but dat dog didn't come. Co'se I knowed he'd come sometime, and so I jes' set dere on dat log and I jes' turned a fool, I reckon, but 'twas jes' lak somebody talking to me, lak it 'peared to me was whispering: 'Josh, you out here in dese woods by yo'self. You blowed dat horn and your enemy heard you. You's a fool, you is.' And I whispered back: 'Dat's a fact.' I couldn't hear what it was a-whispering to me, but us jes' talk back to one 'nuther, and 'bout dat time I look up and here come three men ridin' on new saddles wid shiny buckles gwine, 'squeechy, squeechy', jes' lak dat. I hears de hosses feed jes' as nachel as could be. I thought sho I seed 'em, and it 'pears to look clean outer reason, but dem men come riding right on up to me, and I jump over dat log and lay down flat on de other side, and it look lak I could see right through dat log and heard 'em say: 'Dar he is, dar he is', and I seed 'em p'inting dey finger right whar I was. I knowed dem hosses gwineter step over de log on top me, and I's telling you de troof, I jump up from 'hind dat log and run 'bout two miles, and if it hadn't been for dat slough, I don't know whar I'd a went. I come to myself in de middle of dat water, up to hyar, waist high, and dar was my dog, old Cuba, done treed a 'possum.

"De fust thing I 'members 'bout slave'y time, I wan't nothing but a boy, 'bout fifteen I reckon, dat's what Marse Johnnie Horn say. Us belong to Marse Ike Horn, Marse Johnnie's pa, right here on dis place whar us is now, but dis here didn't belong to me den, dis here was all Marse Ike's place. Marse Ike's gin got outer fix and we couldn't get it fixed. Colonel Lee had two gins and one of 'em was jes' below old Turner house. Recolleck a big old hickory tree? Well dar's whar it was.

"I was plenty big 'nough to drive de mules to de gin. Set on de lever and drive 'em, jes lak a 'lasses mill, so dat night Marse Ike told us he want everybody go wid him to Colonel Lee's gin nex' morning, and didn't want nobody to git out and go ahead of him. Dat held up de ginning; made us not go to de ginhouse tell sunup.

"Us got de mules and jes' waited. 'Twixt daylight and sunup, us all standing dar at de gate and we heared a little fine horn up de road. Us didn't know what it meant coming to de house. And bimeby Mr. Beesley, what live not fur from Marse Ike, he rode up and had five dogs, five nigger dogs, what dey call 'em, and soon as he come, Marse Ike's hoss was saddled up and Marse Ike and him rode off down de road and de dogs wid em, 'head of us. Us followed 'long behind 'em, stay close as dey 'low us, to see what dey was up to. When dey got close to de ginhouse, ginhouse right 'side de road, dey stop us and Mr. Beesley told old Brown to go ahead. Old Brown was de lead dog and had a bell on him and dey was fasten togedder wid a rod, jes' lak steers. He turn 'em loose, and den he popped de whip and hollered at old Brown and told him 'nigger'. Old Brown hollered lak he hit. He want to go. And dey was a fence on bofe sides made it a lane, so he put old Brown over de fence on de ginhouse side, and told Brown to 'go ahead'. He went ahead and run all aroun' de ginhouse and dey let him in de gin-room and he grabbled in de cottonseed in a hole.

"Den somebody holler 'Guinea Jim', I looks and I didn't see him. Didn't nobody see him, but dey know dat's whar he been hiding. Mr. Beesley told old Brown he jes' fooling him, and Old Brown holler ag'in, lak he killing him, and Mr. Beesley say: 'Go git dat nigger' and old Brown started 'way from dar lak he hadn't been hunting nothing, but he went aroun' and aroun' dat gin and Mr. Beesley told him he hatter do better dan dat or he'd kill him, 'cause he hadn't come dar for nothing.

"Brown made a circle aroun' dat gin 'way down to de fence dat time, and he was so fat he couldn't git through de fence. You know what sort of fence, a rail fence it was. Den he stop and bark for help. Now I seed dis wid my own eyes. Dey put Brown on top de fence and he jump way out in de road, didn't stay on de fence. He jump and run up and down in de road, and couldn't find no scent of Jim. You knows how dey used to make dem rail fences?

"Well, Brown come back dar, and dis is de trufe, so help me Gawd. He bark, look lak, for dem to lift him back up on de fence, and bless God, if dat dog didn't walk dat rail fence lak he walking a log, as fur as from here to dat gate yonder, and track Jim jes' lak he was on de groun'. He fell off once, and dey had to put him back, and he run his track right on to whar

Jim jumped off de fence way out in de road. Old Brown run right cross de road to de other fence and treed ag'in on t'other side de road toward Konkabia. Old Brown walk de fence on dat side de road a good piece, jes' lak he done on de other side, and dem other dogs, he hadn't never turned dem loose.

"When Brown he jump off dat fence, he jump jes' as fur as he kin on de fiel' side, lak he gwine ketch Jim lak a gnat or somepin' and he never stop barking no more, jes' lak he jumping a rabbit. Den, Mr. Beesley turn dem other dogs loose dat he hadn't never turned loose, 'ca'se he say old Brown done got de thing straight. And he had it straight. Dem dogs run dat track right on down to Konkabia and crossed it to de Blacksher side. Dey was a big old straw field dar den and dey cross it and come on through dat field, all dem dogs barkin' jes' lak dey looking at Jim. 'Reckley, dey come up on Jim running wid a pine brush tied behind him to drag his scent away, but it didn't bother old Brown.

"When dem dogs 'gin to push him, Jim drap de brush and runned back toward Konkabia. Now on Konkabia dere used to be beavers worse den on Sucarnatchee now. Dey was a big beaver dam 'twixt de bridge and de Hale place, and Jim run to dat beaver dam. You know when beavers build dey dam, dey cut down trees and let 'em fall in de creek, and pull in trash en brush same as folks, to dam de water up dar tell its knee-deep. De dogs seen him, old Brown looking at him, jes' 'fore he jump in 'bove de dam right 'mongst de trash and things dey'd drug in dar. Brown seed him and he jump in right behind him. Jim jes' dive down under de raff, en let he nose stick outer de water. Every once in a while Jim he put he head down under, he holding to a pole down dar, and once Mr. Beesley seed him, he jes' let him stay dar.

"Brown would swim 'bout 'mongst de brush, backerds and for'erds, and terreckly Mr. Beesley tole old Brown, 'Go git him.' Den all de men got poles and dug 'bout in de raff hunting him. Dey knowed he was dar, en Marse Ike had a pole giggen aroun' trying to find him too. Den he told Mr. Beesley to give him de hatchet and let him fix he pole. He sharpen de pole right sharp, den Marse Ike start to jug aroun' wid de pole, and he kinder laugh to hisse'f, 'ca'se he knowed he done found Jim. 'Bout dat time Jim poke he head up and say: 'Dis here me', and everybody holler. Den he ax 'em please, for God's sake, don't let dem dogs git him. Dey told him come on out.

"You see, Jim belonged to Miss Mary Lee, Mr. John Lee's Ma, and his Pa was kilt in de war, so Mr. Beesley was looking out for her. Well, dey took Jim outer dar, and Mr. Beesley whipped him a little and told him: 'Jim, you put up a pretty good fight and I's gwine to give you a start for a run wid de dogs.'

"Jim took out towards Miss Mary's, and Mr. Beesley helt old Brown as long as he could. Dey caught Jim and bit him right smart. You see dey had to let em bite him a little to satisfy de dogs. Jim could have made it, 'cept he was all hot and wore out.

"Dat's 'bout all I knows, 'cept us belonged to Marse Ike Horn, and fust us belonged to Mr. Price Williams, what run de hotel in Livingston. He took my gran'ma to Mobile, den he died. Us Ma belonged to dey two chillun, Miss Nancy Gulley, Mr. Jake's wife, en Miss Burt Blakeney. Marse Ike Horn was dey uncle, and us all come 'round to him, and us been here ever since. My mammy was Ann Campbell, and my pappy was John Horn, and us ain't never had no trouble wid nobody 'bout nothing.

"We's having a barbecue on de fo'th of July and us wants you to come down to it, if Alice gits along well, and I's gwine tell you 'bout Rod and Big John, and John Graverson when dey runned away and about how old man Jim Devers, Alice's step-pa, hid em in de cave under he house whar dey had as nice hams as I ever et, co'se a little tainted, but sho was good. Dem niggers was fat as beavers, jes' settin' dar eatin' dat meat.

"And 'bout de time Marse Ike slip up on a heap of niggers at a frolic 'twixt Sumterville and Livingston and put a end to de frolic. De niggers having a big dance, and Marse Ike and de patterrollers having a big run, said dey wanted to have some fun, and dey did. Said he eased up on 'em wid a white sheet 'round him and a big brush in he hand, and somehow or 'nother, dey didn't see him tell he spoke. Den he holler 'By God, I'm bird-blinding,' and he say dem niggers tore down dem dirt chimleys and run t'rough dat house. He say he ain't never heerd sich a fuss in a corn field in his born days. What he mean 'bout bird-blindin'? When you goes in de canebrake it so thick, you takes a light to shine de bird's eyes and blind 'em, den you kin ketch 'em. Dat what he call bird-blindin'. Yassum, Marse Ike in dat too. He couldn't stand for 'em to have no fun 'thout he in it.

"Come back on de fo'th of July, and I's gwine tell you some sho-nuff tales. You sort of caught me when my min' wa'n't zackly on it. I ain't had no sleep, jes' settin' 'side de bed by Alice, ketching a nod now and den. I's too sleepy to sing you no song, but one I laks is dis: It suits me now in my age:

My lates' sun is sinking fas'
My race in nearly run,
My strongs' trial now is pas',
My triump' jes' begun.

"You come back and I'll sing de res', I's got to see 'bout things now."

Jane

Interview with Jane
—Mildred Scott Taylor, Georgiana, Alabama

DID THEY OWN US OR WE OWN THEM?

"Yas, chillun, I 'members de wah; 'caze I was here when de Yankees come t'rough an' I was about fourteen year ole. Ole Marster he went off to de wah wid a whole passel of sojers, en' he been gone a long time, en' nobody to home to look atter de plantation, 'cep Ole Mistis en' Unker Jude, what was Ole Marster's fust slave he ebber owned. Ole Marster en' Unker Jude was borned de same day, en' Ole Marster's pappy gin Unker Jude to him, whenst dey was leetle bitsy babies. When Ole Marster mai'ed Ole Mistis, dey was young folks, en' dey move to his own plantation. He tuk Unker Jude wid him, en' Unker Jude was de ca'i'ge driver. When Ole Marster went off ter de wah, he tole Unker Jude ter look atter Ole Mistis en' evy'ting on de place 'twell he come back. Whilst Ole Marster gone to de wah, Unker Jude was oberseer for Ole Mistis, en' he made de niggers wuk harder dan Ole Marster did, to make co'n, en' oats, en' fodder, en' meat fer de sojers.

"Ole Mistis made de womens card bats, en' spin en' weabe on de loom. What er loom look lak? It look lak er loom, dat what it look lak; what you spec' it look lak? All de womens, white en' black, wuk hard makin' jeans fer de sojers clo's en' makin' linsey fer de women's clo's. Us didn't hab no udder clo's 'cep dem linsey, but dey sho was good uns en' las' er long time, iffen yer didn't stan' too close ter de fire en' scorch 'em.

"Us kep' hearin' of de Yankees comin', en' one mawnin' Ole Mistis she say: 'Jane, you go down ter de front gate en' stay dar en' watch en' see iffen de Yankees comin' down de big road, en' when you sees 'em, you run tell me quick.'

"Bimeby, I seed de Yankees comin' about a mile down de road, en' I run tell Ole Mistis, en' she call de womens en' dey run down t'rough de orchard to de big woods, en' I run tell Unker Jude en' he onhitch de mules en' lead 'em down ter de big gully behin' de fiel'.

"Ole Mistis tole me to run back to de house, quick, fo' de Yankees get dar, en' git her gole watch en' chain outen de bureau drawer; but de Yankees come in whilst I was gitten de watch en' chain, en' one ob 'em grabbed it outen by han' en' put it in his pocket en' tole anudder Yankee: 'I'se gwine tek dis home ter my gal.'

"De house en' de yard was plum full of Yankees en' dey rid dey hosses en' tore up ev'yting, lookin' for money en' jewelry. Dey ax me whar it was hid, en' I tole em' I didn't know en' dey said I was lyin', en' iffen I didn't tell 'em, dey would kill me 'lak er dam Rebel', en' I sho was skairt.

"Dey et up all de sump'n' to eat in de kitchen en' tuk all de meat en' meal outen de smokehouse en' didn't lef' us nuddin', en' dey went to de crib en' tuk ev'y year co'n en' all de fodder en' put it in wagins en' tuk 'em off.

"De Yankees ax me don't I wanner be free en' I say: 'No, suh', en' dey say ev'body gwine be free an' I won't hab ter wuk fer Ole Marster no mo'. Den dey ax me whar Ole Marster at, en' I say: 'He gone to wah', en' dey ax me whar Ole Mistis, en' I say: 'I dunno whar she at; she done gone off summuz.' Dey ax me whar de guns, en' I tole 'em us didn't hab no guns.

"Dem Yankees mighter been dar till yit, iffen one ob 'em hadn't rid his hoss ober a bee gum en' Man! dem bees en' dem Yankees sho did mess up! In about a minute dere wan't no Yankees nowhar 'cep down de big road whar de dus' jes' foggin' up! 'Bout a week some mo' Yankees come, but dey muster heared 'bout de bees, 'caze dey lef' dey hosses outside de big gate en' walked up to de house, but dey didn't stay long 'caze dey wan't nuffin' lef' atter de fu'st Yankees done to' up ev'ything. En' when dey ready to go dey tuk dey guns en' stood way off en' shoot de bee gums all to pieces, en' dey flewed aroun' en' us had to stay 'way 'twel night. Unker Jude, he wuk all night long, makin' bee gums outen a hollow log, en' nex' day he hive ebery one ob dem bees en' put 'em in de new gums, en' de bees dey tote all dey honey en' put it in de new gums fas' as dey could make comb fer it. Dem bees sho' was smart.

"When de wah done gone, Ole Marster he come, wid one he arms shot plum off, en' Ole Mistis she cry, she so glad to see him en' Unker Jude he cry en' hug Ole Marster, en' us all cry en' tek on, we so glad Ole Marster come back en' so sorry he arm shot off. Ole Marster tell all de niggers dey free now en' don't hatter wuk fer him no mo', en' some er de young niggers went off atter de Yankees, en' neber did come back, but de res' ob us jes' stayed right whar we is. Us had a mighty hard time for a long time, but de white folks had de same hard time en' us didn't mek no diffunce. I mai'ed

Rufus en' us raise a big fambly right dar on Ole Marster's plantation, en' outen us's twelve chilluns, ain't nary one eber seen de inside ob de jailhouse. I raise my chilluns jes' lak Ole Mistis raise her'n en' dat's de way to raise 'em, to wuk en' keep outen debilment. Ole Marster dead en' gone en' Ole Mistis too, but I 'members 'em jes' lak dey was, when dey looked atter us whenst we belonged to 'em or dey belonged ter us, I dunno which it was. De times was better fo' de wah. Us had good things to eat en' plenty of it, en' we had good clo's en' clean clo's fer Sunday. Dat's mo'n some triflin' niggers got now.

"I goes to church en' sings en' prays, en' when de good Lord teks me, I'se ready to go, en' I specs to see Jesus en' Ole Mistis en' Ole Marster when I gits to de He'benly Lan'."

Hilliard Johnson

Interview with Hilliard Johnson
—Ruby Pickens Tartt, Livingston, Alabama

HOODOOIN' DE DOGS

Uncle Hilliard Johnson and his wife Callie live on the Johnson place about three and a half miles from Livingston, Ala., the same place Hilliard was brought as an infant of two in slavery days. He and Callie tend their own little patch of ground and they own a mule. White friends patch up the gaps in their financial structure and everybody knows them. Uncle Hilliard pulled up his mule in front of my house and climbed down from the high seat, leaving Callie sitting placidly in the sun.

He came around to the kitchen door and announced that he was here, "'ca'se he got de word I wanted to ax him somepin."

"Uncle Hilliard," I said, "I want to hear all about you and your family and whom you belonged to in slavery time."

"Well, Miss Ruby, iffen you is knowed me all dese years and still don' know who I'm is, and my family is, and who us belonged to, dey ain't no use of me stoppin' now to tell you. 'Sides, I's sick, I's been to de horspital in York, Dr. Hills', and he wants to operate. I's skeered of de knife and ain't got no money neither.

"I can't eat nothin' but tomato soup. Dem sho' is nice ones you got dere on de she'f, and oyster soup and rice soup and all lac dat. Can't eat no rough vittles lac collards. I ain't gittin' on well atall, but I'll 'blige you a while. I was thinkin' other day 'bout you and dem ole sperichel hymns I leads out to Mount Pilgrim. You's got 'Oh Lord, I'm a Waitin' on You', ain't you? I knowed you had dat 'bout 'And I Can't Do Nothin' Until You Comes. Sho Can't.' Well, here's one you ain't got, 'ca'se hit's a really old sperichel my gran'maw use to sing. I's sorter hoarse today, but hit go:

Jes' carry me and bury me
I'll rise at de comin' day.
Jes' carry me and bury me,
I'll rise at de comin' day.

"Now dat's jes' de chorus and de verse say:

When I was in my worldly ways
Nobody had nothin' to say.
Now I'm ridin' de pale white hoss
Ev'ybody got something to say."

"Den de chorus ag'in, and hit's a pretty one sho's you bawn."

I mentioned the figure of speech "pale white hoss", but he "didn't know nothin' 'bout no figures!"

"And another one, dey is so many, let me see. Here one but I jes' can't call to mine a heap of verses:

Trouble here and dey's trouble dere,
I really do believe dere's trouble ev'ywhere.
Swing low, chariot, I'm gwine home.
Swing low, chariot, I'm gwine home."

"Den hit goes on and tell 'bout de moaner, says:

Oh, dey's a moaner here, dey's a moaner dere,
I really do b'lieve dey's a moaner ev'ywhere.
Swing low, chariot, I'm gwine home.
Swing low, chariot, I'm gwine home.

Oh dey's a sinner here, dey's a sinner dere,
I really do b'lieve dey's a sinner ev'ywhere.
Swing low, chariot, I'm gwine home.
Swing low, chariot, I'm gwine home.

Oh, dey's a Christun here, dey's a Christun dere
I really do b'lieve dey's a Christun ev'ywhere
Swing low, chariot, I'm gwine home.
Swing low, chariot, I'm gwine home.

"Den dey's a heap of 'em to dat song lac a "deacon" and a "member" and a "prayer" and a "singer", jes' a whole passel dem verses, but I reckon dem will do today.

"Now what else you want, 'ca'se dem mules is tired and I is too. 'Sides I got to see a man and Callie in de waggin and she's hot too. You knows Callie, she my wife, my second wife, and us got twelve chillun in all, growed and married. Us still live on de Johnson place three and a half miles from Livingston right han' side de ole Boyd road west from town. Us belonged to Miss Ella Johnson, she was us young Mistis, and Mr. Nep Johnson, dat's de onliest ones I ever knowed. My mammy, Frances Johnson, and my pappy, Alf Johnson, come from down 'bout Cubie Station. Young Mist'iss bought 'em I reckon and my gran'maw, Rachel Johnson. Fus' thing I knowed, us was livin' on Johnson place. Dey was good to us, 'bout seventy-five of us all together, I reckon. All I 'members, dey looped de bridle rein over my feet an' let de mule drag me all over de orchard. It hurt my head. And dey beat some of 'em up scan'lous, but dey was pretty good to me, I reckon. See, I wa'n't so ole, jes' a young boy in slavery time, but I recall young Massa told Tom, a young nigger dere, one time not to go to de frolic.

"'Clean up dem dishes and go ter bed,' he say. And Tom said 'Yassuh' but Marse Nep watch Tom th'oo de do' and atter while Tom slip out and away he went, wid young Massa right 'hin' him. He got dere and foun' Tom cuttin' groun' shuffle big as anybody. Young Massa called him, 'Tom,' he say, 'Tom, didn't I tell you you couldn't come to dis frolic?' 'Yassuh,' says Tom, 'You sho' did, and I jes' come to tell 'em I couldn't come!'

"Young Massa didn't hurt Tom none, but I is seed 'em strip 'em plum nekked and nigh 'bout kill 'em. I did see 'em kill old Collin, but dey done dat wid a shot gun jes' 'ca'se dey couldn't control him. Did they have nigger dogs, you say? Yassum, dey sho' did, but I'm tellin' you de troof now some of de black folks knowed how to git away from dem nigger dogs jes' lac dey wa'n't dere. Mr. Joe Patton, you know Mr. Joe Patton don' you? Young Mr. Joe, I'm talkin' 'bout what's over here in town and use to be de sher'ff. Well, in his day, he done seed a nigger hoodoo dem dogs 'ca'se dey had nigger dogs after S'render too. I kin tell you what I seed, but what dey done now, I doan' know, I couldn't tell you dat. But hit was a fair day, fair as 'tis now, and dey sot de dogs on dat nigger and 'fo' yer knowed hit dat nigger done lef' dere and had dem dogs treein' a nekked tree. 'Twa'n't nobody dere. Dey calls hit hoodooin' de dogs. And I'se seen hit more times than one. Time I tell you 'bout, Mr. Patton was ag'in. 'Twas a feller right here in town. I forgits his name but he was a tall nigger, married Dennis Coleman's daughter. You 'members Dennis Coleman, had dat gal call Hettie? Well, he married Hettie, and he whooped her up mightily. She 'ported on him to de sheriff, and he went to git him. I can't think what dat nigger go by now, but anyhow Mr. Patton couldn't ketch him and he sot de dogs on him and dey couldn't ketch him. Dey knowed whichaway he went, down 'bout Bear Creek on Miss Mamie Smith's place in de flatwoods. 'Twa'n't no trouble to ketch nobody down dere, but dem dogs couldn't do hit, and fus' thing you know he run back to Hattie's.

"Now jes' give me a few tomatoes, Miss Ruby, and I mus' cut dis short. Dey's a cloud comin' up over yonder by Peter's washpot and dat's when us gits a rain. I got a fur piece to go for a old man. Yassum, I'se nigh 'bout seventy-nine years old and porely."

Randolph Johnson

Interview with Randolph Johnson
—Morgan Smith, [HW: Birmingham?]

RANDOLPH AND THE LITTLE CRIPPLE

Randolph Johnson, age 84, although he admits he was "jes' a little picaninny" when the War between the States began, still recalls with vivid clarity the days of his childhood on the old plantation. Unlike most of the former slaves, he never worked hard. His hours were too filled with the joy of playing, for he belonged to a little crippled boy about his own age and guarded over him all the time. At night the little white master and his small black playmate slept in the same room; the latter having a pallet that he spread on the floor. During the day both little white and black played in the shade of the cedars on the grassy lawn. The kindly white owner of the plantation was always good to Randolph. Never a cross word was spoken to him, he says.

"But one day," Randolph said, "de little massa took very sick. Dey wouldn't even let me see him. I had a feelin' trouble was a comin', kaze little massa neber did have no real life like other boys. He was always a lookin' lak a sick puppy. I gues de Lawd jus' wanted him fo' hisself, and he took him.

"Adder dat I was put to work on a mule dat turned de wheel of de cotton gin. He jus' walk aroun' in circles lak de mule dat's pullin' a syrup press. Den de War came, and all de good clothes dat we had made on de loom turned to tatters. De food got low; some of de slaves run away and some of our houses was burned by de Yankees. Atter de war, de massa came back and told us niggers dat we waunt slaves no mo'. Said we could go, but if we wanted to stay we could do dat too. He gib' each fambly dat stayed a mule, a cow, some tools and money enough to run 'em till dey could git de crop harvested. He was de best massa dat any nigger ever had.

"Den I come to Bummin'ham. I worked on de railroad dey was puttin' through. I was a big nigger and I could make de others step. I was about six feet three inches and weighed near 200 pounds. I knowed my ole massa would have been proud of me if he coulda seed me a-workin' on de railroad and a liftn' dem ties and a sweatin' wid dem rails; I wished I coulda been in his cotton field and a-heard him talkin' fair like instid ob listenin' to dat foreman gibin' us de debil 'bout bein' lazy when we was a workin' our selfs nearly to death. Den one day I saw de foreman slap a nigger fo' drinkin' at de dipper too long. De nigger picked up a shovel and slam him in de haid, and run. Back in de slabery days dey didn't do somethin' and run. Dey run befo' dey did it, kaze dey knew dat if dey struck a white man dere want goin' to be no nigger. In dem days dey run to keep from doin' somethin'! Nowadays dey do it and den dey runs."

Emma Jones

Interview with Emma Jones
—Mrs.Preston Klein, Opelika

EMMA TELLS HOW TO MAKE THEM "TEETHE EASY"

Emma Jones, eighty-three years old, was born in the Chattahoochee
Valley between West Point and Columbus Georgia. She is very alert
though quite deaf.

"White folks," she began, "I belonged to Marse Wiley Jones and his wife,
Mistis Melba.

"I lived in a little two-room log cabin with high tester beds and mattreses
filled with cawn shucks. Our food den was away better dan de stuff we
eats today. It was cooked on a fireplace made outen rocks wid big hooks
fastened into de side to swing de pots aroun' on. Us cooked hoe-cakes on a
three-legged skillet dat sot ober hot coals an' us had a big oven for to bake
meat an' cawn bread in. Dere ain't nothin' lak it nowdays, no'm.

"Ole Massa had a big garden an' we useta git de vega'bles we et f'um his
garden. De folks was plenty good to us. Sometimes de mens would hunt
'possums an' rabbits an' wild turkeys. We sho' loved dem 'possums
smothered in 'taters.

"An' talkin' 'bout medicines. Let me tell you a sho' 'nough cure for a baby
dat's havin' a hard time teethin'. Jus' putt a string of coppers roun' he neck
an' he won't have no trouble at all. Us useta do dat to de little white
chilluns an' de black uns too; 'specially in hot weather when dey jus' seem
to have de misery.

"Atter us got to be big gals, us wo' cotton dresses an' drawses in hot
weather, an' when it git col' we had to wear long drawses an' homespun
wool dresses an' home-knitted socks and shoes dat de cobbler made in his
shop. You know, white folks, we useta make near 'bout eve'ything dat wes
needed to run a body raght on our plantation. Us had eve'ything. On
Sunday us wo' gingham an' calico dresses an' I ma'ied in a Swiss dress.

"I worked as a house gal an' when Miss Sarah ma'ied I went with her to
nuss her chilluns. Besides Miss Sarah dere was Mista Billy, Mista Crick,

Miss Lucy and Miss Emma. Dey had two uncles an' a Aunt of deres lived dere too.

"We had a happy fambly. At night some of de house niggers would gather 'roun' de fire, an' mistis would read us de scriptures, an' de white chilluns git tired an' slip out de do' but us little niggers couldn't 'ford to do dat; us hadda stay dere whether us liked it or not. Sometimes de massa let de niggers dance an' frolic on Saturday nights, but we warn't 'lowed to go offen de plantation, none ceptin' de ones dat had a wife or husban' on anudder plantation; den dey could only stay for a short time. Sometimes us could go off to church, an' I remembers a babtizin' in de creek. Some of dem niggers 'most got demselves drowned. Dey warn't used to so much water an' dey would come up outen de creek a spittin' an' a-coughin' lak de debil had a holt of 'em. Dere was so much shoutin' I 'spose ever'body fo' ten miles aroun' could hear dem niggers a-carrin' on in de creek.

"Durin' de war, my mammy helped spin cotton for de soldiers' clothes, an' when de Yankees come through, us hid all de valuables in de woods. Us had to feed dem an' dere hosses too. Dey et up near 'bout everything we had on de place.

"Dere warn't no schools in dem days for us colored folks. Us learned fum de scriptures, an' by listenin' to de white folks talk."

Hannah Jones

Interview with Hannah Jones
—Pigie T. Hix, Greensboro

AUNT HANNAH HAS A HUNDRED DESCENDANTS

Aunt Hannah Jones lives with her daughter in a small four room house on
Tuscaloosa Street, Greensboro. "Lawdy," she said, "It's been so long dat
I's 'mos' forgot 'bout dem slavery days, but I was bawn, in Bunker Hill,
Amelia County, Virginny. My pappy was named Simon Johnson an' my
mammy was Rhoda Johnson. My Marster was Alfred Wood an' my mistis
was Miss Tabby Wood. When Massa died, de 'state was 'vided an' I fell to
de son dat was too sick to take care of de place an' de slaves. Soon I was
tuk to Richmond an' sold to Jedge Moore of Alabammy for twelve
hundred dollars. Dat was de fust time I ever seed a slave sold. I was
sixteen years old. When Jedge Moore's plantation was sold de niggers
went wid de place an' it was bought by Marse Isaiah an' Marse Bill Smarr.
It was called de Gillum Place and dat is east of Prairieville. I was a house
girl an' ho'p wid de sewin' an' de spinnin'.

"Us had good houses built outten cedar logs an' de quarters looked jus' lak
dis street dat I lives on now. We had good beds an' plenty vittels to eat:
greens, cawn bread, meat an' all kinds of sweets. Some time de men folks
would ketch a 'possum or rabbit. Marster had a big vegetable garden an'
we was 'lowed to help ourselves f'um dis here garden. Us had two eve'y
day dresses, an' we done our washin' at night. When I was ma'ied, de
ceremony tuk place at my Mammy's house an' I wo' a pretty white dress.

"Our oberseer was Harvey Williamson an' he went 'roun' at nine o'clock to
see iffen us niggers was in baid. Sometimes atter he done been 'roun', us'd
git up an' have some fun. At de break of day all de slaves would git up an'
go to work. Dose goin' way down in de fiel's would have to git up even
befo' it was light so's to be dar when de dawn broke to commence de day's
work. Den dey would come back at twelve o'clock for dinner an' res'
awhile, den go back an' work till sun down.

"We useta have a man on de place dat played a banjo, an' we would dance
an' play while he sang.

"Dis was one of his songs:

White folks says a nigger won't steal
But I cotched six in my cawnfiel'
If you want to see a nigger run
Shoot at dat nigger wid a gattlin' gun.

"My last Marsters was two brothers an' dey had one sister, Miss Sarah Smarr.

"We didn't have no jail on de place, an' most of us never went offen de plantation, jus' stayed 'roun' an' had a good time playin' amongst ourselves. Us niggers had a church dar on de place an' a white man preached to us, but in Virginny we went to de same church as de Marster did. I didn't jine no church dough till I come to Alabamy.

"None of us slaves ever tried to run away to de nawth 'ca'se dey was good to us.

"We useta have a doctor dat'd come roun' eve'y two weeks to see how de slaves was doin' an' iffen we was sick he would give us some medicine. Some of de women would tie asafetida 'roun' de chilluns necks to keep de sickness away.

"Some Saddays we had to work after dinner, but most of the time Marster would let us have a good time. On Christmas day us had a big celebration an' didn't do no work at all.

"Didn't nobody have no time to learn us how to read an' write.

"I don't know nothin' 'bout Mr. Lincoln 'cep'n he freed all us slaves, an' when we heard dat us was free all de niggers marched to Prairieville an' had a celebration.

"Honey, I's had nine chilluns, twenty five gran' chilluns, twenty seven great gran' chilluns an' thirteen great great gran'chilluns, an' I is expectin' mo' to come along pretty soon. I guess maybee I'll have 100 descendents fo' I shuffle off."

Josephine

Interview with Josephine
—Gertha Couric, Eufaula, Alabama

WHEN SHERMAN PASSED THROUGH

Aunt Josephine claims to be the oldest Negro in Eufaula. She says she was born ninety-four years ago in North Georgia on a plantation above Atlanta. She lives now in Eufaula, Alabama with a great-granddaughter.

"I used to belong to Marse Rogers," she said. "After surrender, Marse Rogers moved to dis country, and bought a plantation 'twixt Marse Josiah Flourney's and General Toney's. He said his plantation j'ined theirs." She was a nurse-maid all of her life, even in Slave days, and never was a "field nigger." Asked if she saw any soldiers during the war she said she saw "thousands."

"I and my Mistis and her baby hid in de swamps three days while Sherman and his army was passin' through," she explained. "Marse Rogers was in Virginny and when he got back home, there wasn't nothin' left but a well. Everything had been burned up. His house was gone and so was de smoke house; everything." She added that the well was a "dry well" where melons and butter and milk and meats were placed, in Summer, to keep them cool.

"Those three days my little brother hid in this well, while the soldiers were passin'," she said.

"'Fore God, Missy," she exclaimed, "when we got dat little nigger out ob dat well, he had almost turned white!"

Aunt Josephine is still a "nurse maid." She rocks her great-great-great-grandchildren.

Lucy Kimball

Interview with Lucy Kimball
—Francois Ludgere Diard, Mobile, Alabama

THE FULFILLED WISH OF MAMMY LUCY KIMBALL

I made two visits to the home of Mammy Lucy Kimball. The first was
during the month of April, 1937; the next was nearly a month later. On the
first trip I had a very successful talk with the old Negro woman, but on the
last, she wasn't at home, and so the information I sought had to wait. I was
very disappointed that I couldn't see her on my second venture, but it was
impossible.

Mammy Lucy had not grown very feeble when I last saw her, and her
methodical mode of living can be attributed to her consciousness of the
venerable age of eighty-five years which she had reached. She was born
into slavery in 1851 at Swift's Landing near the town of Blakeley, in
Baldwin County. She was a slave in the Charles Hall family of that county
before and during the War between the States. In 1907, she came to work
for the T.S. Fry and Santos Rubira families of Mobile.

Following the War between the States, Mammy Lucy Kimball worked in
various families at the summer resorts of Baldwin County.

When a young girl, Mammy Lucy performed the duties of a children's
nurse, and worked as a dining room servant. She had some education, and
as she had worked in families of refinement and culture all her life, her
manner was that of a well educated person. However, like the average
educated Negro, she still displayed the characteristics of the Negro of the
ante-bellum days. She said that she strictly adhered to old fashioned
methods, such as: going to church twice a week, not believing in doctors,
and always taking home-concocted remedies.

I asked her if she believed in carrying a rabbit's foot for luck, to which she
responded:

"Honey, you don' think I'm like these other Negroes, who still believe in
that old nonsense? I might tell the children that a rabbit foot brings good
luck because it is an old custom for superstitions persons to carry one, but,
honey, you'd have just as good luck if you carried brick-bats in your coat.

My white people in Baldwin County never brought me up to believe in such things."

"Well, Mammy Lucy," I asked, "do you remember any strange or weird things that happened during the Civil War?"

"Yes," she answered slowly, "I remember during the Civil War some of the mischievous Sibley boys who were kin to the Hall family over in Baldwin County, tied a strange long black thread to the ankle of a black boy named Slow Poke.

"Some Negroes were going to town that night to fetch supplies and among them was Slow Poke. The boys jokingly asked him if he had his rabbit foot with him as he might need it to keep the rattling noises away at night. Slow Poke showed them his rabbit foot and, displaying his glistening teeth in a broad grin he said that there 'warn't goin' to be no ghosties atter him.' The boys deftly tied a string to Slow Poke's ankle while some of their friends held his attention. On this string were attached three cow bladders. Slow Poke hadn't gone far when he heard the bladders rattling at his heels. He immediately decided that there was a whole troop of ghosts after him, and so began to hit his fastest gait down the middle of the dark road. He ran till he reached Montgomery Hill some miles distant, where the string finally wore out. His people didn't find him till three days later. Then they took him home and gave him a sound whipping for running away."

Mammy Lucy talked of the Hall and Sibley families and of the wealth that they once had, and what happiness she found in being slave to such good people. She remembered all the summer resorts on the eastern shore of Mobile Bay when they were in their glory before the Civil War, and how the Mobile ferries landed bringing over all the fashionable Mobile families to their summer homes on the bay. She remembered hearing father Ryan, the poet-priest of the south, preaching at the dedication of the Catholic Church at Montrose and the storm in the '70's which almost demolished Alabama City (now Fairhope). She recalls the landing of the Confederate troops at Hollywood for wood when they left Mobile at the outbreak of the war on their way to Fort Pickens, Florida, to enter active service.

I found Mammy Lucy to be neat and prim as she must have been thirty years ago, when she first went to work for the Fry and Rubira families. She still walks with the agility of a young person, and her mind is fertile with fresh thoughts and with the deeds of the past. "I have found happiness," she said. "People have been good to me and I, in return, have tried to be kind to those around me. I have lived a plain life and have been rewarded with a ripe age that still finds me feeling young. I shall never grow old in my thoughts and actions, but always keep a place in my mind to welcome something new. I will have had a complete life if I can live only two weeks longer. There is something I'd like to see."

After a few more minutes I left her and returned home. There was something I wanted to ask Mammy Lucy; something that preyed on my mind for days. I wanted to ask her what the thing was that she wanted to see. She was so gentle and courteous; my interest seemed officious prying into her affairs. Someday I shall go to see her again, I decided, and bring up the subject casually. Then she'll never know of my unworthy curiosity.

Three weeks later I walked to the door of Mammy Lucy's cabin and on the porch stood a Negro girl watering a few pots of flowers.

"Is Mammy Lucy at home?" I asked.

The girl was silent for a moment, then she spoke in a high-pitched whining voice: "Mammy Lucy, she died."

"Oh, I'm sorry," I said. "When did she die?"

"Fo' days ago," was the reply.

I walked down the path of pebbles toward the bay. The question would never be answered, but I knew that Mammy Lucy died content.

Ellen King

Personal conversation with Aunt Ellen King
Mauvilla, Alabama
—Mary A. Poole, Mobile, Alabama

SATAN DONE GOT DIS JUKING GENERATION

Ellen King lives in a two room cabin nestling back in the woods near Mauvilla, Ala., about twelve miles above Mobile. A little Negro boy led me along a circuitous path to the ex-slave, showing the weight of her 86 years. After talking awhile she became interested and told that she was born at Enterprise, Miss. on the plantation of Mr. and Mrs. Harvey, but could not recall their given names, or the names of their children, of which there were three, two girls and one boy.

They lived in a big white house and the cabins in the slave quarters were built of planks, with streets between and little gardens in front of them. Some planted vegetables and others flowers.

The Harveys were good masters, they had plenty to eat, and good homespun clothes to wear and home-tanned leather shoes. The women gathered leaves, bark, and indigo to dye the cloth to make their dresses of different colors.

The plantation was large and had several slaves. Aunt Ellen, however, could not recall the number of acres or the number of slaves, but knew there was a crowd of them. The Harvey's raised wheat, cotton and corn, and lots of live stock.

Aunt Ellen sat quiet for a few moments and said:

"Lady, when I sits and thinks of all the good things us had to eat and all the fun we had 'course we had to work, but you knows lady, when a crowd all works together and sings and laughs, first thing you knows work's done."

Aunt Ellen recalled the Yankees coming through and telling all the slaves they were free, and that a lot of the slaves went with them, but Aunt Ellen laughed and said:

"My Pa and some of the others got scared and hid in a big cave and just stayed there until the soldiers left, and, lady, he still stayed on atter the war with the Harveys, and I was married there in the white folks church. They gave me a big wedding, lots to eat, plenty of music, singing and dancing. Jest like they used to say, we 'danced all night to broad daylight.'"

Aunt Ellen was asked how many times she was married and she replied:

"Twice, first one dead and don't know where t'other is, and had no children by either."

When asked about religion Aunt Ellen said:

"Lady, I prayed and prayed and religion came to me, and I jined the Big Zion Methodist Church, in Mobile, Ala., but moved here to Mauvilla where there was no Methodist Church, so I jined the Baptist Church."

Aunt Ellen says the people of today are going back not forward. "All they study is idleness and to do devilment these days. Young generation done gone, Satan got 'am, too much 'juking' these days, have no time to study 'bout the Lord and their dying day. All they do, is juke, juke, juke! When they closed the schools up here in Mauvilla, they had children all juking.

The writer was somewhat at a loss to know just what Aunt Ellen meant by "juking," but thought best to let her talk on and not make a direct inquiry, and after a little Aunt Ellen continued:

"No, lady, we used to call figgers for our dancing, had a big fiddle and two small fiddles, and a set in one room and one in t'other. None of this twisting and turning. I just can't stand all that juking, just won't look at it."

By "juking" Aunt Ellen meant rough dancing of the generation of today.

Aunt Ellen firmly believes the old-time religion was best for all, and tried to sing in a wavering voice the following:

"Down by the river side,
Jesus will talk and walk,
Ain't going to study the world no more,
Ain't going to study the world no more,
For down by the river side,

Jesus will talk and walk."

Mandy Leslie

Interview with Mandy Leslie
—Daphne L.E. Curtis, Fairhope, Alabama

THE ORPHAN SLAVE-GIRL

In the suburbs of Fairhope, in a rough but neatly-kept cottage of two rooms, lives Mandy Leslie, a hard-working Negro woman whose energy belies the seventy-seven years to which she credibly lays claim. Twice widowed and her children scattered to the winds, Mandy is a pillar of strength and comfort to several white households, where she makes weekly calls to care for the laundry work, "wash and iron," as she calls it. The washing is done in the back yards, where a hot fire under an iron pot boils the garments to a state that permits Mandy's rubbing over a fluted wash-board to make them spotless. Strung on lines in the sun, the clothes are ready for ironing next day.

Using old-fashioned sadirons, heated at an open fire, Mandy turns out a "done-up" product that any modern laundry might envy. During the ironing process, which takes place in the hall or a spare room, the mistress of the house is entertained with a steady stream of biography, comment, and information from the lonely old woman who relishes this opportunity to talk to somebody, especially if there happens to be a visitor who is not familiar with her story. A typical episode runs like this:

"Yassum, I 'members de war, but I don't lak no wars. Dey give folks trouble and dey's full of evil doings. When de Yankees come t'rough here, dey took my mammy off in a wagon, and lef' me right side de road, and when she try to git out de wagon to fetch me, dey hit her on de head and she fell back in de wagon and didn't holler no more. Dey jes' driv' off up de big road wid Mammy lying down in de wagon—she mount a been dead, 'cause I ain't never seed her no mo'.

"Unker John Leslie and Aunt Josie and all dey chillun come along in a wagon, gwine up North, dey said, and dey said dey found me standing dar side de road crying for my mammy. Aunt Josie, she say: 'Pore little lamb, you gwine wid us. Us ain't got much, but us can't let you die.' And Unker John, he say: 'Poor chile, us mustn't leave her disaway.' He lift me up in de wagon and drive twell de mule gin plum' out, and den us stop and took up on a place not fur from Mon'gomery, on Mr. Willis Biles' place. Us live dar twell I was grown woman, and Mr. Biles sho' was a good man to live wid and he treat us right every year.

"Den I married Taylor and us kep' on living wid Mr. Biles and all t'ree of us's chillun was borned dere. Den Taylor died wid de fever, and he had insho'ance whet us pay a dollar a mont' for de longest and he say it take care me and de chillun when he gone. Bless God, dat money didn't take care nobody 'cept de doctor and de burying-man. Dey bofe got dey part and lef' me jes' two dollar and seventy cents, dat's all. Mr. Biles say dey ought to be whupped for chargin' me lak dey did. Den he went to see 'em, and cussed 'em out, and dey sont back twenty dollar. I ain't waste no more money on insho'ance, no ma'am!

"I had a hard time keeping my chillun and working de crop too; but Mr. Biles, he 'low me a mule, jes' lak he do Taylor 'fore he died, and us made four bags of cotton de fust year and five bags de nex' year. I pick every lock of it myself—jes' me and dem little chilluns.

"Den Rufus he come along and he thought us had all de insho'ance money, and he court me so hard and so reg'lar dat I act a fool and married him, and he turn out to be de no-countest nigger dat ever lived. 'Stead of him supporting me, us had to support him for nigh 'bout ten year, me and de chillun. He had misery in he back, and couldn't do no hard work lak plowing and hoeing. It hurt he back to pick cotton and pull fodder, and he jes' set 'roun' and make a few baskets and eat lak a hoss.

"Mr. Willis Biles he died, and he boy, Mr. Joe, he took de place and run it for he ma. Mr. Joe told Rufus 'twan't nothing de matter wid him but damn lazy, and if he don't git out and he'p me work, he gonna set de Ku Klux on him. Den us got scared and moved nigh 'bout to Uniontown, and us live wid Mr. Bob Simmons for seben years hand-running, and he treat us right every fall 'bout de settlement. Mr. Bob he say 'tain't nothing de matter wid Rufus jes' lak Mr. Joe say, and Rufus say he gwine move to town whar he kin git work to suit him.

"Us move to town, and Rufus he gone all day looking for a job and don't find nothing to suit him. I has to take in washing from de white folks to feed us and dey charge two dollars rent for de little shack us live in. 'Twan't right to do dat; 'cause I ain't never paid no house-rent in all my bo'n days, twell den. And de fust t'ing I know, dat trifling Rufus he done sell de mule and wagon and got drunk and lost de res' of de money. Us was sho' in a bad fix. Why didn't I quit Rufus? Yassum, I 'spects I ought to done dat; but he' so humble when he sober up and pray so strong. He say de Lord done call him outen he meanness and he gwine preach Jesus. He make lak he need dem preacher clothes, and us skimped along and saved 'nough to buy Rufus de suit of clothes wid a long-tail coat. He got a high-up hat and a Bible, and he sho did look gran'. Us was proud to see him all fix up and going out to labor in de vineyard of de Lord.

"Us give Rufus de las' t'ree dollars us could scrape up and he got on de train and went to Mon'gomery, but us ain't seen hair nor hide of dat nigger sence. In 'bout a year us got a letter from him in Juliet, wayup in Illinois, wharever dat is, and he say he in de pen'tenshry for ten year, 'cause dey 'scuse him stealing a woman's jew'lry, and would I get Mr. Biles and Mr. Simmons to do what dey can to get him out. He repent and been washed in de blood of de Lamb sence he been in jail. And he say if anybody write me dat he runned off from Mon'gomery wid 'nother woman and dat he got a wife in Chicago, it's a lie.

"Dat fix me wid dat triflin' nigger, and Mr. Sam Broady, what's a lawyer, he got me a 'vorcement and gin me back my fust name, Leslie. Now I's t'rough wid marrying. My chillun done all gone and got married, and I come back here whar I come from. 'Twix' here and Brantley, is de place.

"How old I is? I was five year old, come de Surrender—how old dat make me? Sebenty-seben? Dat's right and I be sebenty-eight dis time nex' year. How I know I be living dis time nex' year? 'Cose, I will be living! I always notice dat when I lives t'rough March, I lives de res' of de year, and ain't March jes' now gone, huh?

"How de way wais' ironed suit you, Missy?"

Dellie Lewis

Interview with Dellie Lewis
—Mary A. Poole, Mobile, Alabama

DELLIE LEWIS KNOWS CURES AND 'CUNJER'

"To begin at de beginnin', white folks," said Dellie Lewis, "I was bawn on de plantation of Winston Hunter at Sunflower in Washington County, Alabama. It's on de Southern Railroad. De fus' thing dat I remembers was when de Gran' Trunk Railroad cut dere right of way through near Sunflower. Dey had a chain gang of prisoners dat warn't slaves aworkin' on de road, an' me an' anudder little nigger gal was sont wid big cans of buttermilk to sell 'em. One day a handsome white gent'man rode to our house an' axe me fo' a drink of cool water. He was de fo'man on de road. Jus' as soon as I handed it to him he done fell offen his hoss on de groun'. I run to de Mistis an' she got some of de niggers 'roun' de place to ca'ay de gent'man to de big house, an' do you know it, white folks, dat man, he neber open his eyes again! He keppa callin' de Mistis his mammy, but he neber open his eyes to see dat she warn't his mammy. He died a little later wid a conjested chill.

"Den I remembers one of de Alabama River floods, dat swep' ober de lan' an' washed away lots of de food. De gover'ment sont some supplies of meat, meal an' 'lasses. De barrels was marked U.S. an' one nigger, bein' tired of waitin' an' bein' powerful hongry tol' us dat de U.S. on de barrel meant Us, so us commence' to eat. When de oberseer come to gib us de meat an' 'lasses, us be done et it all up.

"Us slaves useta git up at dawn; de oberseer blowed a cow hawn to call us to work. De Hunter slaves was 'lowed to go avisitin' udder slaves atter work hours an' on Sundays, an' iffen we was to meet a pattyroller, an' he axe us whar we f'um an' who we b'long to all us had to say was we's Hunter niggers; an' dat pattyroller didn't do nothin', caze de Hunter niggers warn't neber whupped by no pattyroller. Some niggers when dey was kotched eben dough dey warn't Hunter niggers, dey'd say it jus' de same, caze dem pattyrollers was always 'fraid to fool 'long wid a Hunter nigger. Massa Hunter, he was somp'n'.

"Durin' de Christmas celebration, us all had gif's. Us had quilting bee's wid de white folks, an' iffen a white gent'man th'owed a quilt ober a white lady he was 'titled to a kiss an' a hug f'um her. Atter de celebratin' we all had a big supper.

"An' speakin' of cures, white folks, us niggers had 'em. My grandmammy was a midwife an' she useta gib women cloves an' whiskey to ease de pain. She also gib 'em dried watermelon seeds to git rid of de grabel in de kidneys. For night sweats Grandmammy would put an axe under de bed of de sick pusson wid de blade asittin' straight up. An' iffen yo' is sick an' wants to keep de visitors away, jus' putt a fresh laid aig in front of de do' an' dey won't come in. If you is anxious fo' yo' sweetheart to come back f'um a trip put a pin in de groun' wid de point up an' den put a aig on de point. When all de insides runs outen de aig yo' sweetheart will return.

"Yassuh, white folks, us useta hab games. Us useta play, 'Puss in de cawner,' 'Next do' neighbor' an' 'Fox an' geese.' I kin gib you some of de songs we useta sing:

Old sweet beans and barley grows,
Old sweet beans an' barley grows,
You nor I nor nobody knows,
Where old sweet beans an' barley grows.

Go choose yo' east,
Go choose yo' wes',
Go choose de one dat you love best,
If she's not here to take her part,
Choose de nex' one to yo' heart.

"I is always been a 'piscopalian in belief, white folks. I ma'ied Bill Lewis when I was fifteen year old in Montgomery an' us had three chilluns. I is strong in my faith.

In mercy, not in wrath,
Rebuke me, gracious Lawd
Les' when Dy whole displeasure rise,
I sink beneath Dy rod.

"Yassuh, I remembers de war. I seed de Yankees a-marchin' through our place an' down de road dat led to Portland in Dallas County. Dey was mighty fine looking wid all dere brass buttons and nice lookin' uniforms. Dey didn't gib us much trouble. Dey had a Cap'n dat was good an' kin'. I heered him say dat dere warn't agoin' to be no stealin' an' atrampin' through folks' houses. Dey slep' outen de yard for one night; den dey went on in to Portland.

"Mr. Munger was our oberseer, but he had money of his own. He was better dan mos' oberseers, an' dere warn't no po' white trash, dem onery buckers libed further back in de woods.

"When us was sick Dr Lewis Williams, who was de doctor of de massa, 'tended to us slaves. I remembers sittin' in de doctor's lap while he tried to soothe my ailments.

"Us house servants was taught to read by de white folks, but my gran'-mammy, Alvain Hunter, dat didn't have no learnin' but dat knowed de Bible back'ards an' farwards, made us study. When me an' my brother was learnin' outen de Blue Back Speller she say:

"'How's dat? Go ober it.'

"Den we would laugh an' answer, 'How you know? You can't read.'

"'Jus' don't soun' raght. De Lawd tell me when its raght. You-all can't fool me so don't try.'

"When de marriages was performed, de massa read de ceremony an' de couples would step off over a broomstick for luck. Den we all had a big supper, an' dere was music an' dancin' by de plenty."

Lightnin'

Interview with Lightnin'
—John Proctor Mills

Ignorant of the date of his birth, which occurred at Cahaba, the old State capital, Lightnin' was an overgrown, gangling youth of fourteen or thereabouts when the Civil War began. Born into slavery, he was the property of one Joel Matthews, cotton planter, whose fields lay near the then new capital city.

Lightnin' is happiest when spinning some yarn of the old days in Alabama for an interested audience, and when one such inquired as to how he came to be called "Lightnin'," the old man broke into a toothless grin and launched at once into another of the stories dear to his heart.

"Dat's Massa Joel's doin's, boss. I jist natcherly wa'nt neber any too peart an fas' on my foots, an de fus' thing Massa Joel eber sot me to fetch him was a cool drink o' water. De water done got wa'm 'fo' I brung it to him, an stid'er scoldin, he jist bus' out laffin' an' say: "Boy, you is so slow I gwineter call you after the fas'est thing on earth. Frum now on yo' name is Lightnin'." An I been Lightnin' eber since. Co'se I knowed Massa Joel was throwin' off on me, lil' as I was, but it looks lak I wa'nt bawn in no big hurry an I jist been movin' long slow-like eber since.

"Massa Joel musta been bawn on a sunshiny day 'cause he sho' was bright an' good natured. Eber' nigger on de place love him lak he was sont from Heaben. Mos' eber' day he come to de quarters wid de fambly doctor to look atter de niggers, fer he say a well-fed, healthy nigger, next to a mule, is de bes' propersition a man kin 'ves' his money in." An' us slaves fared as good as anybody.

"Naw suh! Massa Joel ain't neber hit me a lick in his life. He say a well nigger whut doan' wuhk, sho' ain't got no eats an care comin' his way, an ought'er be sont down de Ribber.

"Is I been mah'id? Yas suh. I done had fo' wives, an raise 'leben chillun. But 'taint lak in de ole days. Chillun all gone, an de ole nigger got no white folks, makes it mighty hahd to git along. 'Bout all de ole man kin do is fish an I does dat an gits a li'l somp'in to eat. 'Fo young Massa Tom passed on—he was Massa Joel's boy—I ain't neber wanted fer nothin'. I was Massa Tom's body guard. Us hunted an fished together, played wid de white chillun an sometimes I rid behin' him on de hoss, or on de fore seat wid de ca'iage driver when de fambly went to chu'ch.

"But dat's all in de pas', an de good Lawd say no man kin bring back de pas'. So I reckon, ef you all 'll 'scuse me, I better go fish my trotline an git somp'in to make the de skillit smell."

Billy Abraham Longslaughter

Interview with Billy Abraham Longslaughter
—F.L. Diard, [HW: Mobile?]

HE CANED A CHAIR FOR PRESIDENT BUCHANNAN

On a bright April afternoon, while strolling along the Louisville and Nashville banana wharf and watching the crisp breezes from the gulf make small waves lick at the pilings, I met an old Negro man who was fishing for croakers off the pier. He had, sitting beside him, a basket containing wicker canes for making and repairing chairs. In the course of our conversation, I asked him his age.

"I'se eighty year old, white folks," he replied.

"Well," I said, "you must have been a slave back in the days before the war."

"Yassuh, boss. I were eight year old when Gen'l Grant freed de niggers." He spoke the words in a clear, strong voice and with a slight rolling motion of his gray bristly head.

"But General Grant didn't free the slaves, Uncle," I protested.

"Oh, yassuh he did too, white folks," he said respectfully; fo' I was right dere when de gen'l come into Richmond and sot us free."

"What about Abraham Lincoln?" I asked.

"Well, I guess he done a part of it, but he didn't do no fightin', kaze he hadda 'tend to de business in de White House. He lef' de freein' part to Gen'l Grant. I don' guess Mr. Abe lived long enough ter help us niggers much. He went to de Ford's Circus and got hisse'f shot."

"What's your name?" I asked.

"Billy Abraham Longslaughter. De niggers all calls me Billy, but ole Massa Longslaughter afore he died called me William."

"Where were you born, Uncle Billy?"

"On ole Massa Longslaughter's plantation near Richmond Virginny."

"Can you read and write?"

"Dey neber teach me no readin' and writin' kaze I had to work in de fields." His rusty hand rubbed across his woolly head, as my questions continued with the regularity of a metronome; nevertheless, Uncle Billy seemed always glad to answer them. I couldn't help but notice with what ease he moved about. He had the agility of a man twenty years his Junior, though his face, being caverned with wrinkles, gave him the appearance of great age.

"Where is your home now, Uncle Billy?" I continued.

"Most any place I goes, white folks. Ma wife, she died 'bout forty year ago in Virginny, and I been a trabelin' eber since."

"What do you do for a living besides fish?" I asked.

"Oh," he said, "I canes a few chairs," pointing to his basket of chair-canes beside him on the stringer of the wharf. "You see, white folks, when all dis repression came on an' dere war'n't no work fo' de people tuh do, jes lak all de young scallawags I hops me a train and goes on a trip."

"Where do you go next, Uncle Billy?"

"Well, I guess I mought run ober to New Orleens if I can catch me a freight train a goin' dat away."

"About your fixing chairs," I said. "Have you ever repaired any for well known people?"

"Lor', white folks, I caned a chair oncet fo' President Buchanan and he used it ter sit on in de White House. I'se made many a chair fo' famous people as I trabeled about. I guess I jus' keep on a goin' as long as I'se able, and when I goes on dat last trip across de quiet riber, I'se goin' ter make one for ole Gabriel, so's he can res' hisself in between times he blows on dat hawn."

Louis

Interview with "Uncle" Louis
—David Holt, Mobile

PSYCHOLOGY OF A RUNAWAY SLAVE

Of course you know that we always called the older colored men "Uncle"
and the older colored women "Aunt." It was proper manners.

Old "Uncle" Louis was the oldest slave on the plantation, "Uncle" Toby
having died. Louis was a "Guinea nigger." His ancestors had been brought
from the Guinea coast of Africa. He had the characteristic marks of his
tribe, being short, strong and very black, with heavy neck, thick lips, flat
nose and eyes like those of a hog. He had great knowledge of wild plants,
claimed to understand the language of birds and beasts. He prided himself
on his powers as a hunter and also claimed intimate friendship with ghosts
and spooks. Being what was known as a "yard servant," he had picked up
much of the talk of his white masters and spoke his own version of their
language.

Old Louis was what was called a "runaway nigger." He would run away in
the latter part of the summer once in every two or three years and come
back in time to help dig sweet potatoes. I was out in the sweet potato patch
one morning when he returned. The doctor was there, also. When Louis
walked up he simply said, "Hello, Louis; are you well?"

"Yes sir, Marster."

"Well, take that basket and go to picking up potatoes." Not a word was
said about his running away. After the hands had knocked off work and
Louis was sitting in front of his cabin, I went to him for an interview.

"Uncle Louis, what makes you run away? You don't get whipped or
abused in any way."

The old slave scratched his grizzled head, puffed at his clay pipe and
pondered the subject for some time before he replied:

"Marse Davie, I does cause de woods seems to call me. When de fall
insec's is singin' in de grass an' the 'simmons is gettin' soft an' de leaves is

beginnin' to turn, I jes natcherly has ter go. De wild sloes, de red haws an' de crab apples is ripe. De walnuts an de hickory nuts an de beach mast drappin' an de blue smoke comes over de woods, an de woods birds an de yard birds goes souf wid de cranes an ducks an wil' geese an de blackbirds an de crows goes in droves—it seem lack all dat is jes callin' me."

"Where do you go?" I asked.

"Lorsy, Marse Davie, I never goes off de plantation. I always go to de woods back o' de past'er. Ole Master knows whar I is an so does Henry. Don't you know dat holler dat come down on de lef' han' side of de branch—de fus holler you comes to, not more dan two hundred yards in de woods?" I knew it well.

"Don't you 'member a big green oak tree growin' on de right han' side of de holler bout a hunder yard up de path?"

"Well, sir, dat tree is my home. I done toted some poles an some sedge gress up dar an made me a bed—but you can't see it from de groun'. When I gets up dar I can see all 'roun'. I seen you an Marse Joe de las' time you go fishin'. I lays dar all day and listen to de birds and critters talkin'. A chicadee tole me you was comin' long befo' I seen you. Den a jay bird caught a sight of you an he tole me. Can't nobody come along widout de birds tellin' me. Dey pays no min' to a horse or a dog but when dey spies a man dey speaks. I done tame' a squi'l so he comes see me ever'day.

"De birds and critters sho is good comp'ny. I done made frens wid up all but de owl and de hawk. Dey is jes natchally bad an de other critters hates 'em. A ole red-breast' hawk come an lit in a daid pine tree. I seen him so plain til I knowed what he was thinkin' about. He was jes mad clean down in his craw and was cussin' ever'thin'. A little pewee bird seen him an begin to fuss. A crow fly over and hear de pewee, den fly down close an take a good look at mister hawk den he fly up and start callin' de other crows. In a little while a whole drove of crows is flyin' 'roun dat pine tree. Den de jay birds come an dey is callin' for a fight, but de ole hawk never move. Den de mocking birds come an dey sair right in and starts pecking at de hawk until he dove into de woods and gets away, an all de birds begin to talkin' 'bout bugs an things."

The old man was wound up for an interminable talk on his favorite theme, the talk of critters, and to change the subject I asked: "Uncle Louis, ain't you afraid of ghosts?"

"Lor', chile, I ain't feared of no ghos' or spook, as I's seed lots of both. All a ghos' do is jes show hise'f. You never hear of one doin' nothin' to nobody. Dey is sociable an wants to be near livin' people. When folks gets scared it hurts de ha'nt's feelin's an dey goes somewhere else. Dey has all de feelin's dey had when dey was livin'. You wouldn't stay by wid folks dat's fear'd of you an want to run away from where you is.

"Las' night, when I was up in my nes', an my fire had died out, all 'sept one little chunk, an de moon was shinin' like day, I lay down, I did, an I take a li'l nap o' sleep. Den I wakes up sudden an looks 'roun ag'in. Well, sir, de norf side of de hill was covered wid ghoses an spooks; dey was layin' down, standin' up and leanin' agin trees, but mos'ly dey was jes sittin' on de groun', all lookin' at me hard as dey could, widout battin' an eye.

"De neares' one to me was a little white ooman. She war sittin' flat on de groun', holdin' a baby in her lap. She look mighty pitiful an I say 'please Missis, can I ho'p you an yo' baby? I'd be 'bleeged if you tell me.' Her lips move but I couldn't hear no sound. Den I lay me down an drap off to sleep agin. When I wakes up de ghosses is all dere an de little white ooman look lak she want to say somethin', but can't, an I say, 'I ain' nothin' but a poor runaway nigger, but my Marster is a mighty kin' man, he'll sholy he'p you; but she didn't say nothin' an I goes back to sleep. De next time I wakes up de sun was risin' an I jes lays dere an watches de ghosses an spooks get thin, an fade away like a fog."

The old Negro was sitting in the twilight, talking in a low, impressive monotone, in a language we both understood but which I find difficulty in transcribing after all these years that intervene. A screech owl was "miseryflying" in the family grave yard back of the quarters, a fitting abligato to the narrative. Though creepy sensations crawled up my spine, I still had my doubts.

"Uncle Louis, do you really believe you saw all that, and didn't dream it while you were curled up in your nest?" I asked.

The old man seemed aggrieved at my doubts as he replied:

"It ain't no beleevin' about it. I knows what I knows an I sees what I sees. De ghos' is what lives when de body is done wore out, but it don't die."

"It's all imagination," I said, in defense of reason and nature, as I understood these things.

"I wants to ax you what does de imaginin'. It's your ghos' that does the imagin' so you can see other ghosses an spooks."

In recognition of Louis' knowledge and powers of reasoning my brother William wrote a diploma in Latin and presented it to him. After that he was called "Doctor" Louis.

I recall that it was about that time that I read a book on psychology but later discovered that there were those on the plantation who had a better working knowledge of the subject than was taught in the book.

Bibliography: Old Plantation Days, an unpublished work by the Venerable David Elred Holt, late Archdeacon of the Sacramento Diocese (Protestant Episcopal) of California, and a native of Buffalo Plantation, near Natchez, Mississippi.

Mandy

Interview with Mandy
—Daphne L.E. Curtis, Fairhope, Alabama

"Howdy Miss. We is sure got a purty day fer de scrubbin' job. Hit will dry as fas' as we turns hit loose.

"Now jes' look a yonder, ef she ain't got gold-fishes an' ever'thing heart could wish!—Is they got ary increases?—Yassum,—dat's good; mebby so you can sell some.

"Me got chillun?—well I is borned three head uv em, but dey all died right now; didn't live a minute.

"Then I 'dopted me a baby boy. A little bitty girl borned him, an' she didn't want him,—he was in her way. She said she'd kill him, an' I didn't want her to git in no trouble, so I tooken him.

"But sho's you bawn I is sorry I done dat t'ing,—dat nigger so triflin', he is goin' on fourteen now, an' he ain't no help to me at all. He only come home when he hongry, an' that's plenty often.

"An' dis yere husbin' whut I is got now, he 'spicions me 'bout other men's all de time, and de boy an' him togedder, keeps ever't'ing riled up mos'ly, twell I'll be glad effen you was to say, you need me to sleep on your place.

"Go to school? Yassum I sho did. I had three months a year for three years, and a extra month onc't, that my mammy paid for. Dat made ten months for me. I was de forwardest chile my mammy had. When dey was any readin' to do my mammy sont fer me.

"Sis Kate kin turn off more work then I kin, but I can mek more cotton. Oncet I won a contest wid a man an' made 480 pounds. Dey gimme a hundred pounds for doin' it.

"Me and Taylor, he's my other husband, the one that died, we used to fo' mek bales near 'bout every year, but dis yer husband whut I got now, he don't do nothin' but jalous me, look lak he'd know I didn' want no man, but jes' fer company; an' dat boy I brung up, he jus' runs nights 'twell I am jes' plumb skeered. So one night I sont for my sister's boy, she is my dead brother's wife, an' Miss, dat rascal, he would steal my las' dime look like. Miss he would steal de har offen your haid could he jus' git a holt, so I jes' sont him back. I talk to him nice befo' I sont him, but hit didn' do no good so I up an' sont him.

"Then Miss Nellie (she that keeps the fillin' station) tooken him an' he stole a whole ginger ale an' a coky coly, an' she cotch him wid em. No'am he didn't git 'em open, effen he had uv, he would uv drunk 'em both, he would fo' sure.

"An' him tellin' folks he married a rich widow. Huh, Mr. Corte he say, 'Mandy you is getting yo'se'f messed for sho'.' He did so Miss, an' he done tole de truf' fo' God, he sho did. I is sho messed up wid 'em bofe.

"But Miss, hit was de bigges' cullud weddin', you ever see, an' me as black as I is. Dey was three tables for de white folks, an' I don' know how many cakes, an' Miss Bessie give me my marryin' dress, an' Mister Harry he give me a dollar, an' him? O yessum, he been married befo', he is got eight head uv chillun. His fust wife's bringin' em up, up in Dallas County, an' him carryin' on like he is down here.

"I allus wanted chillun, a house plum full of 'em, en I done los' all I could mek, so now effen I could of had me some widout 'em I never would of had ary husban' a tall. No'am.

"Me dance? No'am I is j'ined to de Church. Miss Emily she showed me some white folks dancin' oncet, but I thought they was gettin' too closet togedder. In my day they used to swing corners.

"House parties, yassum I is served a many of em. That's what breaks you down, though; day an' night an' day an' night.

"Well, good byc Miss, I surc do thank you for my dollar, an' my cup, an' ever'thing. I is shore enjoyed my day wid you. Me an' you is real good frien's now, ain't we? Hits been jes' like a partyin'.

"Now I'll be gettin' to Sis Katie's, she will mo'n likely want me to carry her Lodge dues up. An Miss, please you ast the bus man, wid yo' telephone, please sir wait for me jes' a minute."

Tony Morgan

From record of a conversation in 1884
—*Francois L. Diard, Mobile, Alabama*

A SLAVE INTERVIEWS A SLAVE

George Washington extolling the virtues of a plain, homespun suit—
granite-jawed Andrew Jackson defying the British at Pensacola—horror
and massacre at Alabama's old Fort Mims—savages skulking near the fort,
their bronzed bodies glistening in the hot August sunlight.

These were among memories of parchment-skinned Uncle Tony Morgan,
who was interviewed on Oct. 1, 1884 by Jim Thomas, another slave, and a
record of the conversation held in the files of a family in Old Mobile,
Alabama. Uncle Tony was 105 years old then.

The story is told by Thomas, former slave of the Diard family. Uncle Tony
was the slave of Mobile Judge H. Toulmin, grandfather of the later Judge
H.T. Toulmin, who was appointed a judge by President Jefferson.

According to Jim Thomas, Uncle Tony told him:

"Did I knowed Gen'l Andrew Jackson? Lord bless you honey, why, I
knowed him and remember Gen'l George Washington afore him."

Uncle Tony explained that he accompanied General Jackson when the
war-loving Tennessean marched from Mobile against Pensacola in 1814.
He said he was serving as a wagoner, and remembered distinctly that the
British surrendered on November 6. He recalled that, during the battle,
Jackson was standing talking with a group of officers when an enemy shell
exploded near him.

"Move away, general," the old Negro quoted one of the officers as saying,
"they'll kill you!"

And Jackson replied in a characteristic manner:

"Damn 'em—I'll have 'em all in hell tomorrow!"

Concerning George Washington, Uncle Tony told Jim Thomas that the great American leader visited the town of Frankfort, Ky., and while there made an address. He wore a home-spun suit, which he pointed out as an example of what people might do in utilizing their products.

Frankfort was highly excited when Washington arrived in the city, and Uncle Tony told of a tiny urchin exclaiming with bitter disappointment in his voice:

"Why, Pa, he ain't nothing but a man!"

Uncle Tony's memory of what occurred at Fort Mims was vivid, according to Jim Thomas. The older slave related that he was one of many Negroes in the fort at the time. He said the defenders had been sleeping off a night of dissipation the morning William Weatherford's warriors attacked.

Men, women and children were butchered in the ensuing slaughter and the buildings were fired. The massacre continued until noon, Uncle Tony said, when the Indians retreated with scalps and several Negro prisoners to their camping site, called the Holy Ground. Here, the half-starved Negroes lived in constant dread that they would be butchered by war-inflamed Creeks.

Uncle Tony also recalled carrying the mail from Fort Stoddert, in Alabama, through the State and Mississippi. On several occasions he barely escaped being scalped by Indians, he said.

The old Negro related further that his father was a wagoner under Cornwallis when that general surrendered to Washington at Yorktown.

Concerning his age and birthplace, Uncle Tony told Thomas he was born in Danville, Ky., about 1779. He went to Mobile in 1805 with Judge Toulmin.

At the time of the interview the old slave was extremely feeble and lame, and walked with the aid of a cane. His skin was dried and wrinkled, and cataracts on his eyes had totally deprived him of his sight. Despite these handicaps, however, Thomas said the old man's mind was exceptionally clear, and his recollection of events occurring almost a century before were remarkable.

Mose

Told by Edith Tatum, Greenville, Alabama
—Mildred Scott Taylor, Georgiana, Alabama

UNCLE MOSE—A TRUE STORY

The early spring sunshine sifted through the honey-suckle vines clustering around the cabin door, and made a network of dancing light upon the floor. A little Negro boy sat on the steps gazing silently up the dusty road and idly listening to the insistent buzzing of insects hovering about the honey-suckle blooms.

"Don't yer see nothin' of her yet, Jerry?" came in a querulous voice from a bed in a corner of the cabin.

"Naw, Unc' Mose. She ain't in sight yit, but it's mos' time fer 'er."

"Hit 'pear lak dis mis'ry is er gittin' wus all de time," the voice went on.

"Miss Sally say dat limerumunt gwine he'p it," essayed Jerry consolingly.

"It don' do no good 'cep'in jess whilst Aun' Judy is er rubbin'. De rubbin' does mo' good dan de limerumunt."

"Dar she is, rat now!" exclaimed Jerry presently.

"Praise de Lawd! fer de ole man sho is hongry en' got de mis'ry from his haid to his heels."

"Dar's ernudder lady wid Miss Sally. Sarter looks lak er gal."

"Mus' be some er ole master's gran'dahters come on er visit. Whyn't yer come an' sit some cheers out an' dus' em' an' straighten dis quilt 'stead er settin' dar lak er black patch on de sunshine? Don' yer know how ter ack when de quality is comin'?" By the time the chairs had been arranged to his notion the visitors were at the door.

"Good morning, Uncle Mose," said the older woman brightly, as she put a covered basket down on a table by the bed.

She had a strong, sweet face and smooth white hair, and the gracious dignity of a queen. "I hope you rested well last night and are feeling very much better. I have brought some one to see you. Now guess who she is," and she placed the girl where the sunshine fell across her face.

Uncle Mose turned his head on the pillow, and gazed eagerly at his visitor. Then his old black face wrinkled into a smile. "Lawd, honey, you sho' mus' be one er Mars' Eddard's dahters, frum de favor!"

"You are right, Uncle Mose. It's Miss Caroline."

"I'm so sorry to find you in bed, Uncle Mose," said the girl, coming closer, while Miss Sally began taking an appetizing breakfast from the basket and putting it on the table.

"Father told me not to come home without seeing Uncle Mose. He talks of you so often."

The old man beamed with pleasure. "Den Mr. Eddard's done fergive me for not choosing him dat time," he said with a chuckle. "Did you ebber h'yar 'bout dat time I choosed mah master?"

"Now, Uncle Mose, none of your reminiscence until Jerry has given you your breakfast. Then I know that Caroline will be delighted to hear all about it," and Miss Sally smiled indulgently. "Here, Caroline, put these flowers in water where Uncle Mose can see them, while I measure some medicine for him."

"Dat sho was er good breakfus', Miss Sally," said the old negro with a sigh of content, as Jerry gave him the last bit of waffle. "Ole Aun' Jincy allers was er good cook, en her ma befo' 'er. Couldn't nobody beat Aun' Lucy cookin' in dem days. Ginger cakes? She made de bes' ginger cakes! Miss Sally, you 'member dat time Ole Marster give me an Mars' Wat er whole silver dollar en we walked two miles to Mars' Walter's sto' en spent ev'ry bit er it fer ginger cakes? Er whole dollar's wuth er ginger cakes, an' Aunt Lucy rat dar at home er cookin' de bes' ones in de country! Mars' Wat sho was er sight!" and Mose lay looking with dim eyes into a happy, long-vanished past.

"Now tell me about when you chose your master," said Caroline, drawing a chair closer to the bed.

"O, dat time; I 'members dat mornin' jess lak it was yistiddy. Hit was in the spring-time lak dis, en ole Mose was er lil' black rascal lak Jerry dar. I was playin' roun' de cabin do' en h'yer come Jim de ke'ge driver, en say ole Marster wanted me rat erway. I sho was skeered! But I couldn't think o' no meanness I had done so I jess helt up mah haid en marched up de road ter de Big House. En dar I foun' Ole Marster standin' on de steps, en in er row on de po'ch was Mars' Eddard, en Mars' Ted, an Mars' Wat, en Mars' Tom. 'Come h'yer Mose,' say Ole Marster in dat big way er his'n. 'Come h'yer en choose yer marster. I'm gwine to give yer ter de one you picks out.' I 'gan at Mars' Eddard. He was older 'en me an' sorter se'rus lak so I passed him by. I looked at Mars' Ted er long time sorter hes'tatin', but den I jess chanced ter look at Mars' Wat, en dem blue eyes er his'n was fa'rly dancin' wid sump'n sorter lak ole Nick, en I say ter mahself, 'dat's de marster fer Mose,' so I say out loud, 'I chooses Mars' Wat,' en bress yer heart, honey, I ain' nebber been sorry er minute sence. But de res' er Ole Marsters' boys nebber did fergive Mose fer dat," and he chuckled at the remembrance.

Caroline laughed. "Thank you, Uncle Mose, I've enjoyed hearing about it. I must go and see Mammy now. Next time I come I hope you will be better."

"De ole man ain' had his foots ter de flo' in five weeks dis comin' Sadd'y Miss Ca'line. Good bye, Miss Ca'line honey, come ergin."

"And now, Jerry, you run tell Aunt Judy to come up at once and rub Uncle Mose's ankles," said 'Miss' Sally as Caroline left the cabin. "I'll warm this liniment and have it all ready." She stopped before the open fireplace and raked up the embers into a little blazing fire, and putting the saucer of turpentine on the floor at some distance, she stood up and turned toward the bed. Just then a spark from the fire fell into the saucer, and the turpentine blazed up. 'Miss' Sally, startled, sprang back, but in so doing, her light cotton morning gown came in contact with the blazing turpentine and was quickly ignited. She caught up her skirts and tried to put it out with her hands, but could not. For several seconds 'Miss' Sally stood face to face with an awful death.

"My God-er-Mighty!" cried Uncle Mose, and with the agility of youth and health he sprang from the bed dragging a blanket with him, and throwing it around her, wrapped it close, extinguishing the flames just as Aunt Judy and Jerry appeared in the door.

"De Lawd in Hebben!" cried fat Judy, her swift glance taking in Miss Sally's white face, burned garments and helpless hands, and 'Uncle' Mose tottering back to his bed.

"Po' lamb! now jess look at dem han's! Lemme tie 'em up in wet sody this minute! You sho 'mos' got burned up, honey."

"I would have, but for Uncle Mose," said 'Miss' Sally faintly, as she sank into a chair.

Aunt Judy turned stormy eyes upon the poor groaning old man. "I'd lak ter know how cum Unc' Mose jess foun' out he kin walk?" she inquired belligerently. "I 'lowed some time ergo dat Mose was possumin'. I sho ain' gwine to waste mo' elbo' grease on dat old hyp'crite."

"Hush, Judy," said her mistress sternly, "Uncle Mose is no hypocrite. He has inflammatory rheumatism. It was a miracle," she added reverently.

"Dat's hit!" exclaimed Mose, eagerly. "Er miracle! Hit was de Lawd-er-Mighty let Mose git up den. Fer how you reckon I'd eber face Mars' Wat ergin' ef I had to tell him I jess lay in de baid en let my lil' mistress burn up? Mose done promus Mars' Wat ter tek keer er Miss Sally, an' ole man done de bes' he could."

Sally Murphy

Interview with Sally Murphy
—Preston Klein, Lee County, Alabama

SLAVERY WAS ALL RIGHT IN ITS PLACE

When I was looking for Sally Murphy, I went into a clean, four room cabin and found a small, neat Negro woman.

"Are you Sally Murphy?" I asked.

"I'm sho' is, honey, and who is you? Lawdy chile, you knows I know Mr. Pompy (my father). She laughed. "I'll tell you anything I knows.

"I was jes' 'bout ten years come slavery done. I was borned down on de Clayton place at Smith's Corners. My pappy he come from South Car'lina, where his pappy was sold. He name was Calop and my mammy was Hannah Clayton. There was eight of us chillun. Fred, Silas, Calop, Mary, Dolphus, Dora, Lula and me. Us all lived down in de quarters, which was five log houses, daubed wid mud. Dem logs was big ones, hand-hewed, and de fireplaces was big, too. Us went to de fiel's early in de morning and picked us a mess of young hick'ry and oak leaves to scald and cook in de pot wid meat. Dey made good greens and us had poke salad, too. (Made from the leaves of the pokeberry).

"When dey dried de fruit us would cook our kind of fruit cake. I don't recollect what went in it. Dere was plenty though. Mistis had de fruit dried on tins in de yard, and at twelve o'clock every day all hands went to de house and turned de fruit.

"Our beds was homemade, scaffold bedsteads wid ropes wove acrost de top what could tighten up. Sometimes us had homewove bedspreads on de beds most every day, but in gen'ally dat was for Sunday only.

"Our menfolks used to hunt possums and wild turkeys, but dey didn't mess 'roun' none wid rabbits. They didn't waste time on fishing either.

"Ev'y morning in May Mistis would call us little niggers to de house and ev'y other morning give us oil and turpentine. We made our own cloth for clothes. Our mammies wove us long drawers outen cotton. Dey bought wool and flannelet to make us pantalets. Us wore homemade homespun dresses. Some of hit was dyed and some checked. Us had shoes reg'lar in winter.

"Ole Marster Joe and Miss Rosa Clayton was good as gold. Dey had Sara, Jane, Henry, and Joe. De live in a big, two story house wid six rooms to hit and had a brick kitchen off from de house out in de yard. Ole Marster had a big plantation and his two aunties live dere, too. Dey was Miss Easter and Miss Charlotte.

"De slave women folks what had chilluns was 'lowed to go home half hour by de sun to wash ev'y day, and ev'y Sunday morning all de little chillun had to be washed and carried to de Big House for de Mistis to inspect 'em.

"Us mostly stayed at home and didn't go 'bout none, and effen us went to Mt. Jefferson Church us had to have a pass or de paterollers would sho' git you. I did think dat 'Hark from the tomb in doleful sound, how careful, how careful den ought I to live, wid what religious fear' was de prettiest thing, and I sho' did love to hear dem sing hit. I never seed de baptising, 'ca'se I used to go to de 'Piscopal Church wid Mistis and open gates and hold de hosses. I sot in de foot of her carriage.

"Christmas dey'd give us provisions and de chillun some trash (meaning toys). Dey sho' had good times on moonlight nights at de cornshuckings. Dey would haul de corn from de fields and put it in a big ring, and as dey shucked dey would throw it in ring and den into de crib. Sometimes dey was so much corn it would stay on de ground 'twell it rotted.

"Mr. Dickey Williams' mother, Miss Emily, ma'ied while us was dere and my grandma cooked de cake. My daddy made de cake stand. Hit had three tiers, each one full of little cakes wid de big cake on top. Hit sho' was pretty.

"Dey let de little niggers have all de fun dey wanted. Us played jump rope and swung in de grapevine swings mostly. Den us had rag dolls. When any of us got sick, we was give hoarhound tea and rock candy. Sometimes effen dey wasn't looking and us got a chance us spit it out. Dey got de doctor effen us needed it.

"One of our Marsters was killed in de war and brought home and buried.
He was Mr. Joe. All de silver was hid out enduring de war but de sojers
never did come to our house.

"One day my daddy says, 'Hannah, Marster said us is free now to do what
we want to do.' But us stayed on two years mo'. In a few years I ma'ied
Milton Heard and had a calico wedding dress and Judge Reed ma'ied us in
Opelika in de ole plank court house. I didn't have no chillun and I lives
now wid my niece, Sally Thomas.

"I don't know what I think 'bout Abraham Lincoln. I don't know nothing
'bout him. Slavery was all right in its place, I guess, 'ca'se some needed it
to make 'em work.

"Folks get so sinful I thought I was safest in de church. I believe God
intended for us all to be religious."

W.E. Northcross

Autobiography of Reverend W.E. Northcross, 1897
—Levi D. Shelby, Jr. (Colored), Tuscumbia, Alabama

(Chapter 1—How Reared)

I was born a slave in 1840, in Colbert County, Alabama. Education was denied me, hence I grew up in ignorance. My mother and father were carried from me when I was only nine years old, but as soon as chance presented itself I ran away and went to them. My white people brought me back, and as they were not cruel to their slaves they did not "buck" me. I stayed with them until I was fifteen summers old. During this time my mistress made all the children, both girls and boys, come to her every Sunday, and she taught Sunday School. The book used was the old fashioned Catechism.

Jesus keep me near the cross,
There's a precious fountain,
Free to all, a healing stream,
Flows from Calvary's mountain.

It was against the law for them to learn to read and write, so she taught them the Lord's prayer and a few other things in the book. She said that she wanted them to know how to pray, how to tell the truth and not to steal, and always try to do right in the sight of everybody and in the sight of God. With these influences, I confessed a hope in Christ at the age of thirteen years.

Am I a soldier of the cross,
A follower of the lamb,
And shall I fear to own his cause,
Or blush to speak his name?

When she did not teach herself, she had an adopted girl to do the same. Finally the adopted girl married and moved to the farm where I was born, the farm from which I ran away. About this time, I was twenty years old. I felt that there was something for me to do. I began to lead prayer meetings. Still I felt that there was more for me to do.

(Chapter 2—Entering The Ministry)

I felt sure that I was called to preach, though "unlearned and ignorant." I trembled at the thought of preaching the gospel, but something seemed to push me forward in that direction. So I asked the people to let me preach. This request was granted. The people at that time had no place or house of worship. I began to fast and pray night and day. Being "unlearned and ignorant" (Acts 4:13) my heart silently murmured—

Bread of heaven, bread of heaven,
Feed me till I want no more.

This was the only school I attended, both day and night. At this time I did not know "A" from "B," but I met a man who could read a little. This man liked me and promised to teach me how to read, provided I would keep it a secret. This I gladly promised to do.

I am weak, Thou art mighty,
Hold me with Thy powerful hand.

I secured a blue-back speller and went out on the mountain every Sunday to meet this gentleman, to be taught. I would stay on the mountain all day Sunday without food. I continued this way for a year and succeeded well. I hired my own time and with my blue-back speller went to the mountain to have this man teach me. The mountain was the great school which I attended. I went from there to the blacksmith shop to work. From that place I was captured by the Yankees and carried to war. As I was crippled I was allowed to remain in the commissary department for about six months. While we were at camp at Athens, Alabama General Forest came upon us and defeated, captured, and killed until they were almost literally wiped out of existence. I had been kind to some little white children, by which I had won their love, and of course, the love of their parents, and stayed with them three days during the battle. I came to a river and turned aside to a farm from which all the people had gone to save themselves from the war, I got a man to help reach an island where I worked three days without anything to eat except grapes and muscadines. I preferred to die on the island than to be killed by the soldiers. Therefore, in time of danger, I rushed to this house and the good people hid me and changed my clothes. Hence, when I was found I was taken for one of the gentleman's slaves. When I was permitted by the man to try to return to LaGrange, and had gone some distance, I was caught by deserters from the Southern army, who voted to shoot me. They bound me and kept me overnight, intending to do away with me the next day. It was a lonely desert on the Tennessee river. I could not sleep, so all night I prayed to God, and the wives of the men prayed to God for the poor "nigger," and also prayed to their cruel husbands. Their prayers prevailed, and I was robbed and let go. I had vowed not to reveal their whereabouts. I left loving God and believing in his providence as I had never believed before.

Earth has no sorrow that
Heaven cannot heal.

I went home and got another spelling-book, although it was not allowed. Some of my own people told my master that I had a book trying to read. He sent for me to come to the house. I obeyed, though I dreaded to meet him, not knowing what the consequence would be. But his heart had been touched by Divine power and he simply told me that he heard that I had a book, and if I was caught with it I would be hung. So I thanked him and departed. Notwithstanding my master's counsel I thirsted for knowledge and got some old boards and carried them to my house to make a light by which I could see how to read. I would shut the doors, put one end of a board into the fire, and proceed to study; but whenever I heard the dogs barking I would throw my book under the bed and peep and listen to see what was up. If no one was near I would crawl under the bed, get my book, come out, lie flat on my stomach, and proceed to study until the dogs would again disturb me. I did this for many nights. I continued in this way to try to learn to spell and read as best I could.

Blessed are they who hunger and thirst after righteousness,
for they shall be filled.

I, like the Ethiopian, wanted a guide. I moved to Mrs. McReynold's. God bless her! She gave me a lesson every night for a period of four years. Then I went to my old master's brother, whose wife helped me every night as long as I would go to her for help. Rev. Shackleford (white) greatly aided me for a period of three years.

Boys and girls, grasp these golden opportunities which are now extended you from the school room. "Unlearned and ignorant" as I was I came along that way until the present time. My readers have better chances than I had. So I hope that they will make good use of their time and make my heart feel glad to see them setting their marks high and preparing themselves for the Great Beyond where all must go. Thither all nations will be called before the mighty judgment seat of the Ruler of the universe to give an account for the deeds done in this world. My prayer for the reader is, that they may make strong, useful, wise and Christian men and women, and at the end of time meet their God in peace.

(Chapter 3—My Work)

I will endeaver, in this chapter, to tell something about my works and whereabouts. I was ordained to the gospel ministry in 1867 by Rev. Mr. Slater (white), and Rev. Henry Bynum. Rev. Stephens Coleman and Rev. Henry Bynum, aided by Dr. Joseph Shackleford (white) laid down the foundation stones for the colored Baptist churches in Morgan, Franklin, Colbert, Lauderdale, and Lawrence counties, Alabama. I am now pastor of the First Baptist Church, at Tuscumbia, Alabama, which is the best Negro edifice in North Alabama. This church was organized thirty-five years ago, by me, with seventy-five members, but it now had a membership of nine hundred. I have pastored it for lo! these many years. This church is an excellent brick edifice. A few other brethren and myself organized the Muscle Shoals Baptist Association—one of the oldest and largest associations in Alabama. I have been Moderator for four years and its Treasurer for six years. I built the church at Russellville, Alabama, and pastored it for four years, and then ordained Bro. P. Jones and recommended him as pastor. I built the Barten church and pastored it for a period of fifteen years, after which I recommended Rev. James Hampton there as pastor. I pastored the Cherokee church five years, ordained Bro. Dennis Jackson and recommended him there as pastor. I pastored Liberty Baptist church for three years, ordained Bro. Alex Brown and recommended him there as pastor. I served Iuka, Mississippi for five years and then recommended a Brother from the West, who belonged to the Mt. Olive Association, to it. I built up the Sheffield church, pastored it three years and then recommended Bro. G.B. Johnson there as shepherd. I also built up Mt. Moriah church at Prides, Alabama. I frequently uttered these words:

Where Jesus leads me I will follow
and his footsteps I'll pursue.

I organized St. Paul church (Colbert County) and pastored it for two years. Rev. E.C. White, who is now Assistant Moderator of the Muscle Shoals Association, was ordained by me. I have ordained more than twenty preachers to the gospel ministry, baptized six thousand persons, united in marriage five thousand couples, and buried about seven thousand persons. I have been faithful to every charge.

Hark the voice of Jesus calling,
Who will and work today?
Fields are white and harvest waiting,
Who will bear the sheaves away?

I have never left the old land mark. Not an one of the churches which I have pastored has brought a charge against me.

The deepest secrets of our hearts
shall shortly be made known.

I have been married three times and have known no woman but my wife, "though unlearned and ignorant." I have never had but one "fuss" with my wife. I told her at one time to hush and she failed to do so, then I slapped her, after which I went to the Lord in prayer and asked to be forgiven. I regret very much indeed to inform the world in print that I have been drunk from intoxicating liquors twice, which was before I professed religion. Notwithstanding I have ever held up temperance and aimed to keep it high until Shiloh comes to gather up his jewels. The following recommendation will show what the best people of Tuscumbia think of me:

Tuscumbia, Ala., March 13, 1897

To whom it may concern:—

We take pleasure in stating that we have known the bearer of this letter, Rev. Wilson Northcross for a number of years, and that he is a conscientious, intelligent colored man of good character. He has been pastor of the Missionary Baptist Church of this place since the war, having been instrumental in building the church, and always has made a good citizen. We believe him in every way worthy of the respect and confidence of his people.

Fox Delony, Judge of Probate
Jas. H. Simpson, Circuit Clerk
Chas. A. Simpson, Deputy Clerk

W.H. Sawtelle
Max Lueddemann

The following resolution was adopted by the church which I pastored thirty years:

Resolved, That Rev. W.E. Northcross, our pastor, is a good, moral, Christian man. He has been our pastor for thirty years, and we can truthfully say that he teaches in all things by example as well as by precept.

--TUSCUMBIA MISSIONARY BAPTIST CHURCH

The history of this church has undergone many changes, but they all worked for its betterment. At the close of the Civil war the few members went from brush arbor to brush arbor for three years. Then they held services in gin houses and under shelters for two years and six months. Then as the church was growing rapidly, they thought best to draw out, buy a lot, and build to themselves. So they bought a lot for what they paid fifty dollars ($50.) and erected a five hundred dollars ($500.) building thereon in which to worship the Lord. So the church continued to grow until it now has a membership of nine-hundred, a splendid brick edifice worth about six thousand dollars ($6,000.) and a thriving congregation. The church has never had but one pastor, and I have been as faithful as a clock. Through me (Rev. W.E. Northcross) the church was built, and I have ever since held high the Baptist doctrine throughout North Alabama.

Roxy Pitts

Interview with Roxy Pitts
—Preston Klein, Opelika, Alabama

ROXY PITTS RECALLS CHILDHOOD

"I don't know 'zackly whar I was born," said Aunt Roxy Pitts, "but it was summuz 'roun Youngsboro, Alabama, en it was in 1855, fo' de wah started, dat Ole Marster said I was born. How ole dat make me? Eighty-two, gwine on eighty-t'ree? Dat's right, en I be eighty-t'ree year ole dis time nex' year, iffen I lives.

"Yassum, I goes to church putty reg'lar, iffen it don't rain; coz de rain makes de mizry in my hip en lays me up. I belongs to de Baptis' church en was baptize wid Jesus when I was twelve year ole. I'se a foot-washin' Baptis', I is, but dey ain't none of dem kind er Baptis' 'roun' here, en I jes goes wid de udder Baptis' en sets in de amen corner, en iffen I wants to shout, I shouts, en nobody ain't gonner stop me, bless the Lord!

"My fu'st marster was name Sam Jones, but I don't 'member him. My udder marster, de one what I 'members, was name Sam Peg, en us lived clost to a little town name Limekiln. My mammy was part Injun, en Ole marster cudden' keep her home ner workin' needer; she alluz runnin' off an stay out in de woods all night long. When I was a little gal, she runned off ag'in en lef' a teeny little baby, en nebber did come back no mo'. Dey said she gone whar de Injuns is. Dat was atter de wah, en pappy had to raise dat little bitsy baby hisse'f. He tuk it en me to de fiel' whar he workin', en kep' a bottle of sweeten water in he shirt to keep warm to gib de baby when it cry. Den Pappy he mai'ed Aunt Josie en dey had er whole passel er chilluns, en dey was my brudders en sisters.

"'Member 'bout de wah? Sho', I 'members 'bout de wah; but us don't hab no wah whar us was. Ole Marster got kilt in Virginny, dey said, en he didn't nebber come back home, en dem what did come back was all crippled up an hurt. Us didn't see no Yankees 'twel dey come along atter de wah was gone, en dey tuk Ole Mistis' good hosses en lef' some po' ole mules, en dey tuk all us's co'n en didn't lef' us nuddin' to eat in de smokehouse. Dey runned off all de chickens dey cudden ketch, en jes' fo' dey lef', de ole rooster flewed up on de fence 'hine de orchard en crow: 'IS-DE-YANKEES-G-O-N-E-E'? En de guinea settin' on de lot fence, say:

136

'Not Yit, Not Yit,' en de ole drake what was hid under de house, he say: 'Hush-h-h, Hush-h-h.'

"Us chilluns sho was misch'us. One time, atter a big rain, us foun' two hens swimmin' aroun' in de tater house, en us tuk en helt em under de water twel' dey's done drownded dead, en we tuk 'em to Mammy en she cooked 'em in a pot en shot de kitchen do'. When dem chickens got done, us went under de flo' en riz up a plank en got in de kitchen en stole one ob dem chickens outen de pot en et it smack up. When Mammy foun' dat chicken gone, she tuk er brush broom an wo' us plum out. But us didn't keer; de brush broom didn't hurt nigh lak de chickens taste good." Aunt Roxy nodded her head and rocked back and forth, as if she enjoyed recalling those youthful escapades.

"Yassum, I kin see plenty good enough to sew, cep'n' I can't tread de needle, en I has to keep atter dese triflin' chilluns to he'p me. You see dis quilt I'se piecin! Miss Lucy gwine gib me tree dollars fer it, coz she say it be made right, en dat's de way I makes em. Miss Lucy know she got er good quilt, when I gits t'ru wid it."

"Is yer got enny snuff, Missy? You don't dip snuff! No'me, I didn't tink you did."

Irene Poole

Interview with Irene Poole
—Susie R. O'Brien, Uniontown, Alabama

HUSH WATER FOR TALKATIVE WOMEN

Under the spreading branches of an enormous fig tree laden with ripe fruit
"Aunt Irene" sat dreaming of old times. At her feet several chickens
scratched and waited for the soft plop of an over ripe fig as it fell to the
ground.

Aunt Irene's back is bent with age and rheumatism, but her two-room
cabin is as clean and neat as a pin. Her small yard is a mass of color where
marigolds, zinnias, verbena and cockscomb run riot, and over the roughly-
made arch at the gate trailed cypress vine in full bloom. "Good morning
Aunt Irene," I said. "A penny for your thoughts."

"Well honey, I don't know as dey is wo'th a penny; not to you anyhow. I
was jes' stud'in' 'bout ole times an' 'bout mah ole marster. You know if he
was livin' today he would be a hundred an' sixteen years ole."

"Who was your master Aunt Irene? Tell me about him."

"His name was Jeff Anderson Poole an' he was de bes' man in de world.
Mah ole miss was name Mollie. I was born on his plantation three miles
from Uniontown eighty five years ago.

"Mah pappy, Alfred Poole, b'longed to Marse Jeff an' he bought mah
mammy, Palestine Kent, from another plantation 'cause mah pappy jes'
couldn' do no work fer thinkin' 'bout her.

"Marse Jeff paid fifteen hunderd dollars for my mammy an' her three little
chillun. Marse Jeff was rich, he owned three big plantations an' Lawd
knows how many niggers. Dey was a hunderd head on our plantation. He
lacked to race horses an' had a stable full o' fine racers. I spec' he made
lots o' his money on dem horses. Miss Mollie say when he win he swell
out his ches' an' stick his thum's in de armhole of his ves' an' talk 'bout it,
but when he lose he don't say nothin'.

"Yas ma'am dere was always plenty to eat. A thousan' poun's o' meat wasn't nothin' to kill on our plantation. My mammy was de cook in de big house an' my pappy driv de carriage an' went 'roun' wid Marse Jeff when he tuck trips. I was a house servant too. When I wasn' nothin' mo' in a baby, de oberseer's wife tuck me to train, so I would know how to ac' in de big house.

"One day she started to give me a whuppin'. Us was out in de yard an' when she bent over to git a switch I runned under her hoopskirt. When she look 'roun' she didn't see me nowhar. After while she started on up to de house an' I runned along wid her under de hoopskirt, takin' little steps so I wouldn't trip her up, till I seed a chance to slip out." Irene threw back her head and laughed loud and long at this amusing memory.

Asked then about her mistress she said: "Yas ma'am she was good. She never punished me, she used to go 'roun' de quarters eve'y mornin' to see 'bout her sick niggers. She always had a little basket wid oil, teppentine an' number six in it. Number six was strong medicine. You had to take it by de drap. I always toted de basket. She gived me mah weddin' dress. It was white tarletan wid ban's o' blue ribbin. I sole de dress las' year but I can show you de pantalets she made me. I used to wear 'em to meetin' on Sunday when us had singin' an' de preacher said words." Aunt Irene brought out the deep ruffled pantalets carefully folded and yellow with age, she had treasured them for seventy-five years.

"No ma'am, Marse Jeff didn't go to de war, I don't know why. I guess it was 'cause he was so rich. Now don't you be thinkin' he was gun shy, 'cause he wasn't an' he done his part too 'cause he took keer o' five widders an' dey chillun when dey men got kilt in de war.

"My pappy lef de night de Yankees tuck Selma. It was on Sunday, an' I ain't seed him since.

"After de surrender us staid on with Marse Jeff. Us didn't keer nothin' 'bout bein' free 'cause us had good times on de plantation. On Sadday dey had corn shuckin's an' de niggers had a week at Chris'mas wid presents for eve'ybody. Camping at de big house an' mo' to eat in one day den I sees now in a year.

"Aunt Irene, do you remember anything about the conjurers in the old days?"

"I don't put much sto' by dem folks. Dey used to give you de han' so you could please yo' mistess an' dey would sell you hush water in a jug. Hush water was jes' plain water what dey fixed so if you drink it you would be quiet an' patient. De mens would git it to give to dey wives to make 'em hush up. I reckon some of de mens would be glad to git some now 'cause gals dese days is got too much mouf."

Sally Reynolds

Personal conversation with Sallie Reynolds
552 South Conception Street, Mobile, Alabama
—Compiled by Mary A. Poole

SATAN'S GOIN' 'ROUND WID HIS TAIL CURLED UP

Sally Reynolds, living at 552 South Conception street, was busy at the
wash tub when the writer called to interview her on July 20, 1937, so it
being a hot day we decided to continue our conversation out doors under
the washshed amid a conglomeration of tubs, buckets, empty boxes, etc.

Sallie said she was born in Hiltown, Georgia, where her mother Margaret
Owens was a slave and the cook on the plantation of Mr. Lit Albritton.
When Sallie was about three years of age her mother gave her to Mrs.
Becke Albritton, who lived at New Providence, near Rutledge in
Crenshaw County, Alabama, to whom she was bound until 21 years of
age. There was also a brother given by her mother to some folks in Florida
and of whom Sallie never had any knowledge whatever.

Sallie said Mrs. Albritton was kind to her, taught her to spin and sew, and
she tried to learn herself to weave, but, somehow, could never master it.

Mrs. Albritton had only a few slaves who were named, Mose, Dan,
Charles, Sandy (the latter so called because he ate sand as a child), and
two women, Hannah and Tene.

They had no regular quarters but just cabins out in a rear lot.

Sallie said all the whippings were given by either of the young Messrs.
Albritton, they were high tempered, as their father was before them. She
laughed and said she had Indian blood in her veins and sometimes she was
sassy as she felt independent knowing Mrs. Albritton would always take
her part.

She recalled the Yankee's coming through after the war, one remained at
the Albritton home after the others had gone on, and she remembered
hearing Mrs. Albritton telling friends who visited her, that after this
soldier had left he wrote Mrs. Albritton a letter, telling her to look on the
back of the bench on the gallery where he had sat and she would find his

message. Sallie said she was a little girl sitting on the floor at her mistress feet, ready to fetch and carry for her and she often wondered but didn't dare ask what the message was; she did, however, hear some one say that the Yankees said, if they ever came again, they would take them from the cradle and that puzzled her, to know just what they meant.

Mrs. Albritton had a regular herb garden and Sallie helped her to gather the herbs, Pennyroil, Dock Sage, Tansy (single and double), Thyme, and Yarrow. They used Samson Snake Root in whiskey for cramps, and Butterfly weed for risings.

The writer asked Sallie about church and she said they had no church but Mr. Albritton talked to her and impressed on her as a child to never touch anything that did not belong to her. "Ask for it and if not given to her, to let it alone and to never lie, or to carry tales, and she could always keep out of trouble." Sallie said she hated to see Sunday morning come, as the men folks were around the house and they would pick on her and somehow she would get a beating.

Sallie remained with Mrs. Albritton until she was 22 years, when she married John Russell, by whom she had three children. They all died as babies, later she married Gus Reynolds, (now dead) so Sallie just rents a room and lives alone.

Sallie says present generation knows too much and too little, that the "Old-time religion" was best for all, she thinks "Satan's goin' 'round wid his tail curled up, catching all he can devour"; and "folks should do like Christ did when Satan tried to tempt Him, and tell Satan to go get behind them, and they get behind Jesus they could not have sorrow run across their hearts and minds."

Gus Rogers

Interview with Gus Rogers
—Mary A. Poole, Mobile, Alabama

JABBO EXPLAINS HIS BLACK SKIN

Living on the Moffat road at Orchard, in western Mobile County, Alabama, on Mr. McIntyre's place is Gus Rogers, who is known better by the name of Jabbo. He claims to be over ninety years of age, but could give no proof. He claims the 26th of June as his birthday.

When asked how old he was, he replied with a smile:

"Miss, I don't know but I found everything here when I came along."

He was born at Salisbury, N.C. on the Rogers' plantation, and Mr. John and Mrs. Mary Rogers were his master and mistress. His parents were William and Lucy Rogers, who had five children, three girls and two boys.

Jabbo said the Rogers's home was built of boards of virgin timber and the slave quarters were some distance from the big house. Some of the cabins were built of logs and some of boards, all having clay chimneys and big open fireplaces equipped for cooking, as the slaves usually cooked their own meals, except during busy seasons, when meals were prepared in the house kitchen by the slave women too old to work in the fields.

Jabbo said one old man went around and rapped on the doors to wake up slaves to go to work. When asked how long they worked he laughed, and said:

"Just from sun to sun and then you went to bed, 'cause you knew that old man would sure be rapping before you were ready next morning."

When asked about earning any money, Jabbo said:

"Law, Miss we didn't even know what money was, and we didn't have no use for it. We had all we needed, plenty to eat and all the clothes necessary those days."

The Rogers raised lots of tobacco and wheat, and all the necessary farm products needed on the plantation. They had a large orchard and made all the cider they could drink.

Jabbo recalled driving many a refugee wagon during the War, and when they heard of the Yankees' coming, the Rogers family took all the horses and mules and hid them in the swamps and buried all the silver and other valuables.

After the devastation wrought by War, Mr. Rogers moved his family to Massey Station, Montgomery County, Alabama, intending to raise cotton. He brought Jabbo's father and mother and family with him, but meeting with little success he returned to Salisbury, N.C. Jabbo remained in Alabama.

Jabbo married and raised a family of five children. There were two girls and three boys but he has no knowledge of their present whereabouts.

When asked if he was married more than once, Jabbo laughed and said:

"No, Miss I always had the price of a marriage license in my pocket, but somehow I never married."

In answer to inquiry as to religion, Jabbo replied:

"Miss, I am a Methodist, but there's only one religion. You have to be pure in heart to see Him, because He said so, and to do unto others as you desire others to do unto you."

Continuing about religion Jabbo said:

"God gave it to Adam and took it away from Adam and gave it to Noah, and you know, Miss, Noah had three sons, and when Noah got drunk on wine, one of his sons laughed at him, and the other two took a sheet and walked backwards and threw it over Noah. Noah told the one who laughed, 'you children will be hewers of wood and drawers of water for the other's two children, and they will be known by their hair and their skin being dark,' so, Miss, there we are, and that is the way God meant us to be. We have always had to follow the white folks and do what we saw them do, and that's all there is to it. You just can't get away from what the Lord said."

Jabbo said he would like "to go back to the good old days, 'though there was good folks and there was mean folks, then too, just like there is today."

Bibliography: Personal interview by the writer with Gus Rogers, ex-slave, better known as "Jabbo."

Janie Scott

Personal interview with Janie Scott
255 South Lawrence Street, Mobile, Alabama
—Mary A. Poole, Mobile, Alabama

SLAVE CA'LINE SOLD FER A SACK O' SALT

Janie Scott, living in a cottage at 255 South Lawrence Street, was interviewed by the writer on July 14th, 1937. She claimed she was born April 10, 1867, but she appeared older than seventy years of age. She, of course, was unable to give any experiences of her own as a slave but recalled what had been told her by her mother, who was a slave on the Myers plantation at Tensaw, Alabama.

When asked how large was the plantation, Janie answered:

"Lordy, chile, many an acre an 'bout sixty slaves."

Her mother worked in the house, and when the field hands were working helped carry water out to them in buckets, each one getting a swallow or two a piece. Her father was Andy White, and was raised on the plantation of John Jewett at Stockton, Alabama.

Janie had heard her father say he was a coachman and drove the folks around, also came over in a boat with his master to Mobile to get supplies and groceries, and that they killed many a deer in neighborhoods just north of Bienville Square.

Jane said her mother's Master and Mistress didn't want her mother to marry Andy, because he was too light in color and light niggers Janie said folks didn't think as strong as a good black one, so her mother, Sarah Porter, and Andy White her father just borrowed a mule without the Master's consent and rode off and were married, anyhow.

Janie laughed and said she guessed it was all right after all because they had eleven children, two are now living, Janie and a sister Daisy.

When the writer asked if slaves ever earned any money, she replied:

"They didn't even know what money was." Then she continued: "Once when my mother was a little girl she asked her mistress to give her fifteen cents, and her Mistress wanted to know why she wanted fifteen cents. Her Mother replied: "I wants to see what money looks like."

Her Mistress thought she was trying to act smart and in place of fifteen cents she received a whipping.

The slaves wore homespun clothes, but her mother remembered having as her best dress one made of marino.

The slaves quarters were log cabins with clay chimneys, and they cooked in the open fireplaces in the winter and in the summer on what they called scaffolds, built out in the yard. These were made of clay foundations with iron rods across on which the pots hung.

Janie said her mother "was strong and could roll and cut logs like a man, and was much of a woman." Then they had a log rolling on a plantation the Negroes from the neighboring plantations came and worked together until all the jobs were completed.

After each log rolling they gave them molasses to make candy and have a big frolic.

During the Civil War when supplies were scarce, especially salt, Marster John rode off taking her mother's sister Ca'line with him, and when he returned alone his wife, Mrs. Meyers, wanted to know where was Ca'line, and Marster John replied: "I sold her for a sack of salt." At first they did not believe him, but Ca'line never returned and Sarah never saw her sister anymore.

After the Surrender the Yankees came through and the slaves hid under the house, but the soldiers made them come out and told them they were free, and gave the slaves everything on the place to eat. They all went down to the creek and praised God for what he had done for them.

Janie does not believe in charms, hoodoo or fortune-tellers, saying:

"Those folks can't tell you nothing. When Christ was risen He carried all prophets with Him and didn't leave any wise folks able to tell things going to happen here on earth—everything Christ wanted folks to know had already happened."

Janie did say the best charm she knew of was a bag of asafetida worn around the neck to ward off sickness or to take nine or ten drops in a little water would sure keep the worms down.

The slaves got plenty of coons, rabbits and bear meat, and could go fishing on Sundays, as well as turtle hunting.

The overseer on the Myers plantation was not a mean man, they had a calaboose or sweat box to punish unruly slaves in place of whipping them.

After the Surrender her father and mother moved to Mobile, Alabama, and her father continued to work for Mr. Jewett at his mill located at the foot of Palmetto Street on the Mobile river front.

John Smith

Interview with John Smith
—Susie R. O'Brien, Uniontown, Alabama

"MAD 'BOUT SOMEPIN'"—SO THEY HAD A WAR

John Smith is 103 but he doesn't want to be tied down. "Effen I's free, I wants to 'joy it," John says, and he lives up to his desire. Though he is a "war veter'n" with bullets in his side and leg and his century of life has enfeebled him, he roams the countryside about Uniontown continually, "settin' a spell" with his acquaintances.

It was only after several trips I finally caught him "settin'," and he showed no inclination to move from his advantageous position near a watermelon patch. He was industriously working on a huge slice of melon, his face buried in the sweet fruit, as I drove up to the little cabin where he was visiting.

As the car came to a stop he raised his head and wiped his dripping chin on his sleeve. He called to a little Negro girl in the yard, "Gal, go bring de white lady a rockin' cheer", and turning to me he said, "You'll 'scuse me for not gittin' up lak I ain't got no manners, won't you Mistess? I got a misery in my laig; you know de one whar I got shot in de war."

The rocking chair was brought out and taking a seat nearby I said, "Uncle John, I want you to tell me all about yourself, were you in the war and are you really a hundred and three years old'?"

"Glad to, glad to mistess, but fust don't you want a watermillon?" He pointed to a patch nearby where the melons glistened in the sun. "Dis July sun make de juice so sweet you'll smack yo' mouf for mo'," and searching the rind to see that he had left none of the juicy red meat, Uncle John began his story.

"Well, I been livin' 'roun' dese parts 'bout ninety year. I was born somewar in North Ca'lina, I don't 'member much 'bout my Mammy an' Pappy 'cause I was took 'way from dem by de speckerlaters when I was 'bout thirteen year ole. De speckerlaters raised Niggers to sell. Dey would feed 'em up an' git 'em fat and slick and make money on 'em. I was sold off de block in 'Speckerlater's Grove' in North Ca'lina. De fus' day I was put up I didn't

149

sold, but de nex' day I brung a thousand dollars. Mr. Saddler Smith from Selma bought me. Dey called him Saddler Smith cause he was in de saddle business and made saddles for de army. Dey fotch us down on boats. I 'member de song de men on de boat singed. Hit go like dis:

Up an' down de Mobile Ribber,
Two speckerlaters for one po' lil nigger.

"My marster was de best in dis country. He didn't had many niggers, but he sho' tuck good keer o' dem what he did had. He didn't 'low nobody to hit 'em a lick. Sometime when I would git cotch up wid in some diverment de white folks would say, 'Whose nigger is you?" and I say, 'Marse Saddler Smith.' Den dey look at each oder an' say kinder low, 'Better not do nothin' to ole Smith's nigger. He'll raise de debil.'

"I didn't had no mistiss. My marster was a widder. He raised me up workin' 'roun' de saddle shop. I ain't never liked to work nowhow, but don't tell nobody dat. I was bout twenty seven year ole when de war broke out. De ole uns was called out fust and de young uns stayed home and practiced so dey could shoot straight an' kill a Yankee. Us practiced every Friday evenin'. Course I didn't know what dey fightin' 'bout. I jes' knowed dey was mad 'bout somepin'. Atter while Marster's son Jim j'ined de 'Federate sogers an' I went wid him for to tote his knapsack, canteen and sichlike and to look atter him. Dat's when I got dese here balls in my side and got a bullet in my laig, too. I was movin' de hawses to de back of de lines out de thick of de fight when, zipp, a minit ball cotch me right in de shoulder."

Proudly John displayed the balls in his side and the scar on his leg. The old woman, at whose cabin John was visiting, interrupted the story several times. Finally he got tired of it and said: "Shet yo' mouf 'oman, I don't need no ho'p, dis is grown folks talk, you don't know nothin' 'bout it, you wasn't even birthed tell two year 'fo' de Surrender. Now whar was I at? I slep' right by Marsa Jim's side. Sometime atter us done laid down and bofe of us be thinkin' 'bout home, Marse Jim say, 'John, I lak to have some chicken.' I don't say nothin' I jes' ease up an' pull my hat down over my eyes an' slip out. Atter while I come back wid a bunch o'chickens crost my shoulder. Nex' mornin' Marse Jim have nice brown chicken floatin' in graby what I done cook for him. Us was fightin' on Blue Mountain when Marse Jim got kilt. I looked and looked for him but I never did find him.

Atter I lost my marster I didn't 'long to nobody and de Yankee's was takin' eve'y thing anyhow, so dey tuck me wid dem.

"I tuck keer of Gen'l Wilson's hawse, Gen'l Wilson was de head man in de Yankee army. But I didn't lak dey ways much. He wanted his hawse kep' spick and span. He would take his white pocket hankercher an' rub over de hawse and if it was dirty he had me whupped. I was wid Gen'l Wilson when he tuck Selma 'gins't Gen'l Forrest and sot fire to all dem things. I drive de artillery wagon sometime. Atter Surrender I was kinda puny wid de balls in my side."

"John," I asked, "why didn't they remove the balls at the time you were shot?"

"How could dey 'move de balls when I was runnin' fast as I could pick up my foots? I driv de stagecoach twixt Selma and Montgomery. I 'member my stops. Dey was Selma, Benton, Lown'esboro and Mon'gomery. I driv four hawses to it. Dere was a libbery stable at Benton and I changed hawses dere."

"Now John tell me about your wife and children," I said. "How many children did you have?"

"Gawd, I don't know mistess. Dey runnin' 'roun' de country like hawgs. Dey don't know me an' I don't know dem. I ain't never been mai'ed. Niggers didn't marry in dem days. I jes' tuk up wid one likely gal atter anoder. I ain't even mai'ed to de one I got now. I jes' ain't gwine tie myse'f down. Effen I's free, I's gwine to be free."

Uncle John sat for a time in deep thought, then said, "I wish I mought be back in dem days, 'cause I been seed de debil since I been free. Atter I was free I didn't had no marster to 'pend on and I was hongry a heap of times. I 'long to de 'Federate nation and always will 'long to y'all, but I reckon it's jes' as well we is free 'cause I don't b'lieve de white folks now days would make good marsters."

Uncle John had about talked out and as I rose to leave I said, "Thank you John, this will make a good story," to which he replied indignantly, "Hit ain't no story. Hit's de Gawd's trufe mistess."

Annie Stanton

Personal interview with "Aunt Annie" Stanton
Rylands Lane, Mobile, Alabama
—Ila B. Prine, Mobile, Alabama

Out on Ryland's Lane is an old negro woman 84 years of age who is totally blind, but whose mind is clear in regards to things pertaining to the long ago.

"Aunt Annie" says that things that happened when she was a child are much more vivid in her mind than are things of today. She said "Sumtimes I now starts tuh do dumpin' an' fogits what I wants tuh do, den I ahs tuh go bac' tuh de place whar I started from so I kin 'member whats I started tuh do".

"Aunt Annie" was born on Knight's Place on the Alabama River, June 2nd., 1853. This place is now known as Finchburg, in Monroe County, Alabama. Her mother's name was Mary Knight and her father's name was Atlas Williams, who had the same name as his owner, Mr. Offord Williams. "Aunt Annie's" mother's people were owned first by Mr. Cullen Knight and after his death, were owned by Mr. John Marshall.

"Aunt Annie" was seven years old then the Civil War started, and that she had "nursed two cullered chillun afore de war."

When asked by the writer about nursing these children, so as to be sure she said colored children, she replied, "dat de slaves lived on de plantation, and dey had an overseer who libed on dis place, an' she neber seed de Marshall's place 'til after dey was freed. As I growed bigger into a big yearlin' gal I was tuk intuh de oversee'rs home to 'tend tuh de dinin' room table sich as settin' hit an' washin' de dishes an' cleanin' up, an' later on I was showed how to iron, spin thread, weave cloth, and make candles. Honey, folks talkin' 'bout depression now don't kno' nothin' 'bout hard times. In dem days folks didn't hab nothin' 'ceptin' what dey made. Eben if yo' had a mint ob money, dere was nothin' to buy. We made de candles to burn by tying strings on the stick and puttin' dem down in melted tallow in moulds. In dem times we had no matches, folks made fire by strikin' flint rocks together an' de fire droppin' on cotton. I don't know whether dese rocks were ones dat de Indians lef' or no, but day was dif'rent from other rocks. People usta carry dem an' de cotton roun' in boxes sumtin lak snuff boxes tuh keep de cotton dry. Sumtimes when dey could'nt get de fire no odder way, dey would put de cotton in de fireplace and shoot up in dere an' set hit on fire."

"Aunt Annie" said she never could start a fire with the flint rock and cotton, and she said, "de fust matches and lantern I'se eber seed was when de Yankees cum tuh dere place, I th'ot dey was two officers, 'couse dey had de matches and lantern. Two years a'ter I was freed, an' twar den I seed mah first lamp.

"De men did mos' ob de farm wurk, dey planted cotton, corn, potatoes, cane, peas and pumpkins, an' dey ginned de cotton by hitching four horses tuh de gin, and dey run hit dat way."

When asked if they had plenty to eat when they were slaves, "Aunt Annie" said:

"Lor', yes I guess we had 'nough, but, 'tearn't much, c'ase I 'members when we was li'l chillun we had a big wooden tray dat dey put de food in and we all set 'round dat an' et like li'l pigs. De rations for a week was 3 lbs of meat a week, 1 peck ob meal, potatoes an' syrup. At Christmas times de overseer called all de men an' women in an' gib each woman a dress, a head handkerchief, an' tuh de men he gave a hat, knife, an' a bottle of whiskey. De overseer also gib tuh us flour and sugar fo' Christmas, an' I 'members one Christmas when I was a li'l gal, a'ter de overseer gib all de women a dress dere was a short piece ob cloth lef' an' he gib dat tuh me." "Aunt Annie" said "dat de slaves went tuh de white folks church, an' sot on de seats on de outside ob de church, an' dat church was a hewed log building. Atter de white folks got thro' preachin', den de cullered preacher would preach. Sumtimes de cullered folks would hab church when de white folks didn't an' den de slaves would hab tuh get a pass from his owner, 'ca'se dere would be some mean folks what would beat de niggers ef dey didn't hab a pass from dere owners or bosses."

"Aunt Annie" also said, "I'se neber hyeard of no hoodoo stuff 'til in late years, dey's mo' ob dat foolishness now dan I'se ebber hyeard of in mah life. Nowadays de hoodoos doctors, what is allus agoin' 'round foolin' folks out ob dey money, looks lack de dogs might ob and' dem, dey is so turrible lookin'. I don't believes in dem. Us folks a long time ago neber hab no money fo' dem to git. Us had tuh make own medicine. When de babies had de colic us wud tie soot up in a rag an' boil it, and den gib dem de water, an' tuh ease de prickly heat us used cotton wood powdered up fine, and fo' de yellow thrash us would boil de sheep thrash an' gib em de tea."

"Aunt Annie" has been married twice, her first husband left her years ago, when she married Louis Stanton and had five children by him. Louis was killed in a hailstorm, April 13, 1903, and all of her children are dead. She is now being cared for by friends, and she said, "that ef I's didn't git a li'l he'p from de Government tuh gib dis frien'" she didn't know what she would do as she has been totally blind for two years.

9 781976 465130